THE GREAT LIVERPOOL BLITZ

RICHARD WHITTINGTON-EGAN

Gallery Press

Leighton Banastre, Parkgate, South Wirral.

ISBN 0 900389 27 3
Published by Gallery Press 1987
© Richard Whittington-Egan
Printed by Scotprint (North West) Limited.

The Liverpool Dossier Series
All titles in this series were originally published
in Richard Whittington-Egan's earlier books
LIVERPOOL COLONNADE and LIVERPOOL
ROUNDABOUT.

Now available:–

Back in the days when the Beatles would still pop into Ye Cracke in Rice Street to take a friendly ale with me, I was paying a young man's court to the fickle jade of the Mersey. I wrote two love chronicles of our on-off affair—*Liverpool Colonnade* and *Liverpool Roundabout*. Oh, I was a knight-errant then, pricking in fancy my milk-white palfrey through the stone forest and down the avenues of my imagination. And such imaginings! I saw the Liver birds take wing against a low lying hunter's moon . . . the chimney-masted tangle of sky-riding roof-tops looking at dusk like the decks of ships at swaying anchor . . . I heard the golden and porcelained names on windows singing the old crafts' songs and lullabies of trade . . . I lurked around the Western bazaar counters in the lit grottoes of the shops . . . I rode the overhead railway and the Noah's Ark tramcars . . . watched the glittering city slip over the horizon's edge into the purple pomp of night—and out again into the watered-milk light of another dawn. Both I and the Liverpool of which I wrote have grown up, grown different. We have played weather-vanes to the wind of change. And yet we are still the same at heart. The fresh wind blowing across the river and over my city's wild hilltop still whispers the old tales to those who are willing to listen . . . a light still burns in Paradise Street . . .

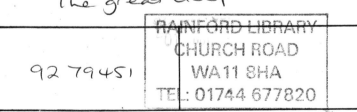

WHITTINGTON, Egan

The great Liverpool Blitz

1 THE NIGHT THEY TRIED TO BURN LIVERPOOL

May 1st, 1941.

That date belongs to history, for that was the night that history was written in letters of fire across the Mersey sky. It was the night, too, that ushered in what was probably the worst week (up to that time) that the world had ever known.

Many years have gone by since then and still the full story of all the horrors and splendours of those seven soul-shattering nights has not, until now, been told. Years during which a new generation has grown up that knows nothing of its home-town's terrible ordeal by fire. A generation for whom a blitzed site simply means a conveniently clear stretch of waste land upon which to play a game of football. A generation to whom that ominous gap in a row of terrace houses has no more significance than as a useful short cut to the shops. For these young people the sound of an aircraft passing overhead is part of the pattern of life. Even the rush and scream of a jet evokes no more than the admiring craning of a neck, whereas for those older ones amongst us who lived through the fearful years of Hitler's *blitzkrieg* such innocent sounds vibrate deep chords of memory and, just for a split second, fire-bright pictures come crowding into our minds.

May 1st, 1941, was a Thursday, and shortly before 11 p.m., just as the men and women of Merseyside were preparing to go to bed, the dismal keening of sirens sounded on the still night air. It was a nuisance. Tired workers clambered back into their clothes. Sleepy eyed children were snatched from their cots. With a shrug, mother put the kettle on. It was going to be another late night. Weary, red eyed people filed into the shelters. It *was* a nuisance, but folk had grown used to that sort of thing in those days. It seemed to them that it was just another routine raid. What they did not - could not - know was that to-night was different: to-night was to be the fiery prelude to a fugue of fear in seven searing episodes. What they did not - could not - know was that on Hitler's desk in Berlin there lay that night a memo

7

addressed to the Führer by Herr Raeder, and in that memo were the significant words:

"An early concentrated attack on Britain is necessary, *on Liverpool for example,* so that the whole nation will feel the effect."

This memo was the direct result of the failure of Goering's Luftwaffe to defeat the R.A.F. which, together with certain bickerings which had for some time been taking place between the German Military and Naval High Commands, had led to the continued postponement of the proposed invasion of Britain. Faced now with his Secret Service's warnings of the ill-omened entry of the Soviet Union into the war, and thoroughly frustrated by the lack of effective co-operation between his war leaders, Hitler began seriously to consider Raeder's plan to starve Britain into submission by the cutting of her imports.

Great Britain, being an island, must obviously in time of war rely to a very considerable extent upon the streams of weapons, munitions, raw materials and food-stuffs, which flow to her ports across the seas of the world. Paralyse her ports and you effectively cut off her vital supplies. That Liverpool could not be closed to traffic by submarine warfare alone had become apparent early in 1940, and now, growing rapidly more and more desperate, the Führer decided to implement Raeder's suggestion and hurl the full fury of his Luftwaffe into a determined effort to put the Port of Liverpool out of commission.

All of this came to light, of course, after the war, when British and American intelligence officers captured the German naval archives and amongst them the minutes of what were known as the "Führer Conferences," and back in May 1941, neither the British Government nor the man in the shelter had the slightest suspicion that Liverpool was about to become Number One Target.

From the number of planes operating that night-there were about 50 of them - it looked at first as though an exceptionally heavy-scale onslaught might be expected, but, due it is believed to deteriorating weather conditions on the other side of the English Channel, the attack suddenly faded out and the raiders scuttled for home.

The first bomb was dropped on Wallasey at 10.50 p.m., and for some time at the beginning of the raid only the roar of a heavy anti-aircraft barrage could be heard, and the black velvet of the sky was spattered with the sequins of bursting shells.

Then, suddenly, a rain of hundred of incendiaries began to fall and, between their flickering focuses of fire, the heart-fluttering thud and thump of high-explosive bombs began to tremble the earth.

All in all, that first night was not an outstandingly bad one, judged by the standards of those explosive days. There were rather less than 100

incidents in Liverpool and none at all in Bootle. What damage there was was heavy rather than widespread. Low Hill and Cazneau Street suffered, and the North Market, the roof of which was in process of being repaired after being damaged in a previous raid, was hit again. Batty's Dairy in Arundel Avenue, Sefton Park, was struck. The proprietor, his son and 19 cows were buried under the debris and one cow was blown into the roadway where a policeman ran into it on his bicycle in the darkness.

A bomb which blasted the front from a wholesale tobacconist's provided a passing docker with an opportunity to exercise that 'scouse' sense of humour which even Hitler's high-explosives never succeeded in demolishing. He looked at the broken relics of thousands of those then rare luxuries and said laconically, "If it's not pubs it's cigarettes Jerry goes for!"

And there was the usual crop of freak incidents such as the saving of the James family by a piano. The blast from a nearby bomb blew in the front portion of the house, but the family, who were lying in bunks in the dining-room, were protected by the piano in the parlour, which stood against the dividing wall and bore the full brunt of the blast.

A woman's intuition saved the 5-year-old son of a Mr. and Mrs. Hamilton. The boy was sound asleep upstairs and all at once his mother became strangely uneasy. Without a word, she rushed up to his room and carried him downstairs. Almost the moment she re-entered the lounge there came a terrific crash from upstairs. Several large lumps of concrete had come bursting through the bedroom window and smashed the bed where, sixty seconds before, her child had been sleeping.

Not quite so happy is the story of a Mrs. Gladys Cooper and her daughter, also Gladys, who had only recently come to 44 Avondale Road, Sefton Park, after being bombed out of their home in another district of Liverpool. The two women usually sheltered under the stairs, but on this particular night they decided that they would go out into the corporation domestic shelter at the back of the house. Unfortunately, the shelter received a direct hit and they were both killed. The house was also severely damaged but, by one of those ironic twists of fate, the stairs still stood, and had the Coopers been beneath them as they generally were the odds are that they would have been perfectly safe.

At 1 a.m. the 'All Clear' sounded and Merseyside went back to bed. There were still several hours to go to dawn, but the sky was already bright with the reflection of the fires. Fires which even now the Fire Service was battling to quell, but some of which would still be burning to-morrow night, pointing red fingers along the bombing run to what the communiqués called "a North-Western Port," when for the second successive night the Luftwaffe came to try to crush the brave heart of Liverpool.

2 THE TERROR THAT FLEW BY NIGHT

"Last night enemy aircraft again attacked a North-Western Port. The attack was heavy and lasted several hours."

The newsreader's voice on the radio was clipped and matter-of-fact as the words in which the Air Ministry and Ministry of Home Security communiqué tersely dismissed Liverpool's second night of hell. Merseysiders exchanged meaningful glances across their breakfast tables, switched off their wirelesses and went out to pick their way to work across the steaming piles of rubble which were the legacies of the worst raid, so far, of 1941.

From 10.20 p.m. on May 2nd until nearly 3 o'clock the following morning, wave after wave of enemy bombers had swept across the sky and raked the earth with incendiaries and high-explosives. "The attack was heavy and lasted several hours"! It didn't seem much of a tribute to a stricken city: it seemed, in fact, quite a masterpiece of understatement. Still, no one felt more than a passing pang of resentment on that score for, after nineteen months of war, everybody was alive to the vital importance of maintaining a thick security blanket. Indeed, only now is it possible to lift the corners of that blanket and take full stock of the awful events that crowded a nightmare week made hideous by the terror that flew by night.

Statistics are cold things, they cannot tell us much of the living anguish which went to their making, but nevertheless the following figures, which show the tragic toll of that merciless week in May as compared with the total number of civilian casualties sustained throughout the entire blitz, are quietly impressive:

LIVERPOOL			BOOTLE			BIRKENHEAD			WALLASEY		
Casul-ties	All Raids	May Blitz	Casual-ties	All Raids	May Blitz	Casual-ties	All Raids	May Blitz	Casual-ties	All Raids	May Blitz
Killed	2,596	1,453	Killed	460	257	Killed	464	28	Killed	355	3
Injured	4,148	1,056	Injured	1.426	26	Injured	661	44	Injured	909	19

During that single week 800 raiders dropped 2,000 bombs and started 1,200 fires on Merseyside. As the damage mounted the housing position became critical. In Liverpool, Bootle and those parts of Litherland and Crosby which fringe it, 90,000 houses were damaged and destroyed, a total which represented about 40 per cent. of all the houses in the area concerned. In Bootle alone, which, in relation to its size, endured the most concentrated attack of anywhere in the British Isles, no less than 80 per cent. of its houses were damaged and 25,000 people had to be found alternative accommodation. To make matters worse, more than three quarters of those rest centres which had been expressly designed to cope with just such an emergency had been put out of action. Birkenhead's dwellings also suffered to the tune of 25,000 out of a possible 34,000. In Wallasey 7,500 persons had to be evacuated from their shattered homes and the civic authorities in Liverpool found themselves with practically 51,000 homeless people on their hands.

By the end of that week the billeting position in the Merseyside area had become absolutely impossible and special emergency measures were being taken to send people, at short notice, to a number of nearby reception towns.

Truly, that fateful week brought the front line to Merseyside - into your street.

Night after night, police, ambulance drivers, rescue parties, the women's volunteer services, wardens and many other civil defence personnel worked valiantly amidst the smoke and smother. Firemen went several days without so much as taking off their uniforms and, after snatching a hurried cup of tea from a mobile canteen, volunteer civil defence workers went straight from a sleepless night on the battlefield of the streets to important daytime jobs keeping the production lines moving in the factories.

Hour upon hour, the raiding planes buzzed and droned like flights of angry hornets over the river, and death and destruction came whistling and screeching from the flare-lit sky.

Hundreds upon hundreds of buildings sagged and crumpled, or else reared up into a million bursting fragments - shops, business premises, dwelling-houses, blocks of tenement flats, cinemas, theatres, schools, hospitals, pubs and churches.

And as the week drew to its close, the sneering affected voice of Lord Haw-Haw mouthed one of the foulest of all his slanderous lies: "There are riots in Scotland Road and the south end of Liverpool. People are marching around with white flags and shouting for peace." That, about a city whose charwomen never failed to turn up at their early morning work even though the trams stood immobile on their twisted rails and it often meant a very long walk from their homes in the suburbs: that, about a city whose citizens made a special point of getting to the office as usual on the morning after their homes had been blasted to pieces. And the tragic thing is that the soft mocking voice of Hamburg was spreading Hitler's lies all over the country. "Bryant and May's Bootle matchworks has been flattened by the German Luftwaffe," it announced triumphantly, "and a thousand workers have lost their lives." Actually the factory *had* been hit, but not a single person was killed there. But the security blackout had to be maintained and no one rose to contradict the lying claims of propaganda. Whatever the rest of the country might be thinking, we here on Merseyside knew that, thanks to the simple courage, the faith and the heroism of the people, the worst that the German Air Force could do was temporarily to slow down the activities of the port.

May 2nd, 1941, was a night of bright moonlight; the sort of night that fills the mind with moonbeam thoughts of poetry and of love, but sixteen years ago there was only hatred, and we saw the moon not as the peaceable lamp that lights romance, but as a beacon for disaster. And so indeed it proved, for by its rays close on a hundred bombers throbbed their way to our blacked-out city.

The raiders concentrated that night on the city centre. For practically four hours the whirlwind havoc wiped out time-honoured landmarks. The Dock Board Building was hit. A large fire was started in the old White Star Building. Church House, South John Street, in which were situated the offices of the diocese of Liverpool, was gutted, and valuable records and books went up in a glaring bonfire. Famous St. Michael's, the Anglican church of Chinatown, was irreparably damaged, and that night saw the beginning of Bootle's ordeal, with a savage attack on Balliol, Knowsley and Bedford roads, and 200 people rendered homeless.

It was in that raid, too, that the Liverpool Corn Exchange was razed, and the following morning the members met to transact their business in the street. That was typical of the indomitable spirit of Liverpool. The spirit of a people who, with wry humour, could chalk up outside a shattered shop, "Removed during alterations." People who, somehow or other, managed a smile in the face of tragedy. People like the old gentleman who was following his wife at the double towards the Anderson shelter in the garden when that lady shouted, "Bill, do go and get my false teeth. I've left them in the bedroom." Just then a bomb whistled perilously close, and as it exploded with a dull roar Bill yelled back above the noise, "What do you want them for? They're dropping bombs, not ham sandwiches."

You know, you can't crush that sort of spirit, but there was to be more - much more - to try it, and the following night was to see a crescendo of horror and terror rarely, if ever, equalled in the annals of human suffering. The miracle is that Merseyside could and did take it.

3 A SATURDAY TO REMEMBER

Saturday is one of the most sacred institutions of our British way of life. It is traditionally a joyful day. A day when the cares and worries of office and workshop are put aside. A day for watching football matches. A day for playing cricket. It is a day for taking the wife to a show and perhaps having a little convivial glass afterwards.

But Saturday, May 3rd, 1941, was cast in a very different mould. It was a day straight from the most outrageous pages of H.G. Wells. It was the day when Liverpool took the most harrowing pummelling in the city's 700-year history from a great armada of something like 500 Nazi bombers. Night fighters and a spectacular barrage bagged a record total of 16 enemy planes, but nevertheless so terrible was the damage wrought that one scarcely knows where to begin in trying to assess the six or seven hundred incidents which, between the hours of 10.30 p.m. and 5 a.m. that night, reduced a proud city to a charred and steaming waste of bricks and mortar.

At one stage in the night so many fires were blazing that it really seemed as if the whole city was alight and the tower of the cathedral was floodlit by the red glare. The tally of famous buildings damaged and destroyed reads like a guide to Liverpool.

In peacetime the very idea of a fire at Lewis's is something terrifying to contemplate, but when, just after midnight, stick after stick of fire-bombs and high-explosives hurtled down onto its roof, transforming, in a matter of minutes, its entire seven stories into a roaring hell, it was just another 'incident'.

The fire from Lewis's spread rapidly to Kelly's, the ironmonger's, and, a few yards away, Blackler's Stores suddenly burst into flames. The blast of earlier bombs had already shattered many of its windows, and the wind blowing through their glassless gaps fanned the flames. Due to the bursting of the mains, there was a most unfortunate shortage of water in that area with which to combat the fire and a frustrated N.F.S. had to stand by practically helpless while Blackler's was reduced to a blackened skeleton.

Everything in the shop was destroyed - not a single object was salvaged - and among the £200,000 worth of stock lost was a consignment of fully-fashioned, sheer silk stockings which had only arrived a day or two before and was valued at something like £10,000. The loss of that item alone was sufficient to break the heart of the most stoic Liverpool lady, for at that time silk stockings came high on the list of under-the-counter luxuries.

Across on the far side of the city, fire-watchers saw a 500 lb. bomb fall on the William Brown Library. In the mammoth fire which ensued all the volumes on the shelves of the Central Lending Library were lost, the entire Music Library went up in smoke and a large portion of the stock of the Picton Reference Library perished. In all about 150,000 volumes, valued at something in the region of £126,000, fed the hungry flames.

The wind swept the fire next door to the museum (which had already had a bomb or two of its own) and, with the exception of the lower horseshoe gallery , it was entirely gutted. There was plenty of fried fish in the aquarium in the basement that night, and Sammie the Seal, who had delighted thousands of Merseyside youngsters, became surely one of Liverpool's strangest air-raid victims!

The adjacent buildings of the Walker Art Gallery and the Technical College did not escape undamaged, and wool and tobacco warehouses in Pall Mall and Highfield Street, Cheapside oil and fat works and the Salvage H.Q. in Hatton Garden were all badly hit.

The General Post Office in Victoria Street was struck for the second time and put completely out of action, so that for a period business had to be carried on from the Fruit Exchange.

Bank and Central Telephone Exchanges were demolished and the resultant dislocation somewhat impaired the efficiency of the civil defence services. Some very fine work in re-establishing lines of communication was done, however, by post-office engineers and service linesmen, who between them fixed up miles of temporary, overhead wires.

Blazing fragments blowing in through bomb-blasted windows gave rise to a large number of separate fires in India Buildings. Among the offices which were more or less totally destroyed were those of the Inland Revenue. Later, when most of the fires had been extinguished and the building had cooled down, an inland revenue staff officer went to the special strong-room in which certain all-important records of your and my incomes were kept. To his delight he found that the fire had not penetrated the fireproof doors.

Unable to contain himself in his unholy glee, Mr. Bloodsucker ran off to tell his colleagues the glad news, but in his excitement he left every door open behind him. The draught which resulted caused some still-smouldering material to burst anew into flames and the contents of the strong-room were irretrievably lost!

With the burning of the Cook Street Arcade, the Law Society mourned the loss of its 35,000-volume library.

The most fearsomely concentrated devastation took place in an area embracing Paradise Street, Lord Street, South John Street, South Castle Street, Canning Place and Hanover Street. Not all of the buildings in this rectangle received direct hits, but fires spread rapidly and gutted many that had not been bombed at all.

A particular tragedy was the severe damaging by fire of the old Bluecoat Building, a beloved centre of Liverpool's cultural life.

The biggest single incident of the night was the blowing up of the *Malakand*. S.S. *Malakand* was a steamer of the Brocklebank Line, and she was lying in Huskisson Dock No. 2 with 1,000 tons of shells and bombs for the Middle East in her hold. Somewhere about 11.15 p.m. a large and partly deflated barrage-balloon, which had been torn from its moorings, became entangled with the ship's rigging, fell onto the for'ard deck and promptly burst into flames. Within fifteen minutes the crew had put the fire out, but meanwhile a shower of incendiaries and several high-explosive bombs had fallen on some neighbouring dock sheds and the flames from one of the sheds had soon enveloped the *Malakand* from stem to stern. At this juncture Captain Howard Cooke Kinley, who was on duty as shore relief master, gave the order "Abandon ship!"

For many hours all hands fought desperately from the quayside to scuttle the *Malakand* and prevent a terrible explosion. The danger was very great but, with absolute disregard for their own safety, Captain Kinley and his crew, together with A.F.S. Officer John Lappin and a handful of A.F.S. personnel, struggled on. But all their efforts were of no avail, and a few hours after the 'All Clear' had sounded Merseyside shook to one of the greatest explosions of the entire blitz. The whole dock was demolished. Stout stone walls crumbled to dust. The Overhead Railway line and station were badly damaged. Some of the ship's plates were recovered 2.1/2 miles away. One of her 4-ton anchors was blown more than 100 yards onto the top of the engines of a dock Board hopper. Captain Kinley and several men were injured, but only four persons were killed, two of whom were a married couple motoring home along the Dock Road when a huge fragment of steel plate fell onto their car. A Dock Board employee, picking a careful way between broken carboys of acid in an adjoining shed at the time of the explosion, had a narrow escape. He was thrown to the ground, where he found himself beneath a side plate from the ship which, blown off and badly buckled, was covering him like an Anderson shelter.

Beyond the boundaries of the Dock Estate, Bootle itself was having a bad time, too. With 200 homes totally demolished, 400 seriously damaged and a further 3,000 slightly damaged, there were few streets that escaped. The Town Hall, Bootle Cold Storage, Johnson's dye-works, Vernon's pool offices, the gas-works and a number of timber-yards all sustained damage. Williams's toffee-works and Scott's bakery were gutted.

Fifty-seven people were killed in Bootle that night and one of the most tragic occurrences was the direct hit which razed St. Andrew's Hall, which was being used as a rest centre, killing all twelve of the W.V.S. members who were busy caring for the homeless.

Nor was drama lacking, for at Mill Road Infirmary a young Greek seaman named Dutches was actually on the operating table in the basement theatre undergoing an urgent operation for abdominal trouble when it was completely wrecked by a bomb. A nurse - Miss S. George - who had been assisting at the operation, managed to struggle out of the debris and led rescuers to a window through which they were able to climb in and rescue both the patient and the surgeon. The interrupted operation was successfully completed at another hospital. The bomb which fell in the courtyard at the back of the infirmary was of exceptionally heavy calibre and it completely demolished three large hospital buildings. Seventeen members of the staff, 14 ambulance drivers and 30 patients were killed outright; 70 people were seriously injured and 380 patients had to be trasferred to other hospitals. Doctor Leonard Findlay, the medical superintendent, and the matron, Miss Gertrude Riding, though themselves injured, displayed great gallantry which was subsequently rewarded with the George Medal and the O.B.E. respectively.

Such then was Saturday, May 3rd, 1941 - a night of unmitigated horror. Things were bad - very bad. They might have been worse had it not been for the selfless devotion to duty of all those who fought the terror of the clouds. They seemed tireless - the police, the firemen, the wardens, the doctors, the ambulance men, the civil defence workers of all the services.

Their vigilance saved Liverpool. One tiny incident exemplifies the zeal - in this case amusingly misplaced - that defeated the worst the German Luftwaffe could do. A policeman and his wife were doing battle with an incendiary which had come crashing through the roof into a bedroom and had set some furniture alight. The policeman was crawling forward, a stirrup-pump in his hand, playing water on the bomb, when suddenly from outside came a warden's loud and angry voice: "Put that bloody light out. Don't you know there's a raid on?"

4   SUNDAY IN RUINS

When Merseyside awoke on the morning of May 4th, 1941, it found that a curious change had taken place in the shape of Sunday. It was not so much the silence of the church bells, because for many months now they had hung mute, their music conscripted to provide a clangorous warning if invasion took place. But many of those bells would never ring again, for last night the bombs had toppled them from their steeples. Indeed, churches seem to have been among the principal targets of that dreadful Saturday and the handful of weary crumpled church folk who dragged themselves to Divine Service that morning found, all too often, their parish church blasted to a grotesque pile of rubble, or else took their seats in stark shells bereft of that softly-coloured twilight which once filtered through stained-glass windows.

Nevertheless, the services still went on at churches of all denominations. In one Roman Catholic church, for instance, which had been ruined by fire, the Holy Eucharist, Communion vessels and vestments were salvaged, and the priest made hurried arrangements for Mass to be celebrated in the adjoining church hall. Significantly, one of the few remaining and recognisable features of the church was a stone tablet of the Crucifixion which stood out undamaged among the ruins.

But that was only one facet of a changed city. A city whose streets were blocked with tumbled masonry, carpeted with a million million shining splinters of broken glass and braided with miles of snaking rubber fire-hoses. Liverpool had never looked like this before. The very air seemed somehow altered. It was sharp and acrid. It stung the eyes and tweaked the nose. Over everything there hung a pall of smoke and dust, and a black blizzard of burnt paper from stricken shops and offices blew across the Sunday-morning city and was swept out on the breeze to remote suburban gardens.

17

Within the city itself was a scene of the utmost desolation. Everything was in a state of chaos - untidy with spilled bricks and sullen smoking fires. The defence services faced an urgent task. It was vital that as many of the fires as possible should be put out before evening came again. It was equally vital that the streets should be cleared so that A.R.P. and rescue vehicles would not be hampered when the battle was resumed. Every second of daylight was precious.

Throughout the day, the Fire Service, augmented by firemen sent in from 39 Lancashire, Cheshire and North Wales towns, fought the stubborn flames, whilst more than 6,000 demolition and clearance workers - including 2,680 troops who had been drafted in for the purpose - plied hook and crowbar to the demolishing of dangerous ruins, and wielded pick and shovel in an all-out effort to clear the roads.

The work of demolition, as opposed to that of road clearance, was the responsibility of the City Building Surveyor and he was greatly assisted in this emergency by the military. In many instances normal methods of demolition were useless and explosives had to be resorted to. This was something entirely new in the city, and the demolition squads received invaluable help and advice in this novel form of demolition from a number of Lancashire mine engineers. A company of paratroopers stationed in the area also lent a hand, gaining useful practical experience in the process. The hundreds of thousands of tons of building-debris resulting from all these operations required rapid removal, and a great deal of mechanical plant, in the form of excavators and diggers, and hundreds of lorries, in which to transport the material to tips, were employed in this task. At one time when, because of exceptionally heavy raiding, operations were being held up for lack of mechanical plant, a mechanical section of the American Armed Forces which had just arrived in Liverpool was contacted, and the Colonel promptly sent along two of the largest mechanical excavators ever seen in this country, together with a number of service personnel to man them.

It ultimately transpired that this plant had never before been used, and the soldiers were not at all sure how to operate it. The first shovel-load lifted was of such immense weight, and was released from so fearsome an altitude, that the lorry waiting to receive it was forced wheel-deep into the soft earth. Nevertheless, the soldiers, most of whom were gentlemen of colour and smoked cigars all day long, seemed to be thoroughly enjoying themselves and, once they had got the hang of their complicated equipment, proved themselves excellent workers.

As the day wore on, many Merseysiders thronged the streets to view the enormous damage of the Saturday night, thus impeding the work of the services. An appeal was made for people to keep away from the scenes of damage, and this was emphasised by the Lord Mayor who, while paying a tribute to the spirit of the people, spoke of a Sunday throng "like crowds at Blackpool, in streets we are trying to keep clear."

The sustained attack on the Merseyside area had by now become nationally recognised, and an urgent call brought a fleet of the Queen's Messengers' Convoy here from Manchester that Sunday within an hour and twenty minutes. The convoy included a water tanker, a kitchen lorry, a food store and two mobile canteens, one of which, presented by the Queen herself, had its baptism of fire that morning, with remarkable escapes by its crew. Driven by Miss Lily Griffiths, of Romiley, Cheshire, with Donald Dewar, of Leicester Road, Bootle, as messenger, and accompanied by Mrs. Wilson, Mrs Blackhurst and Mrs. Woolrich, the vehicle ran into the thickest of the raid. A bomb fell right beside it, splinters shattering the windscreen and penetrating the roof of the driver's cab right over Mr. Dewar's head, while others ripped through the offside door and crashed through the chimney. Part of the convoy was based on Liverpool itself, and from midday on Sunday, 3,000 sandwiches, 3,000 cups of tea and 3,000 bowls of soup were served to hungry fire-fighters, civil defence workers and bombed-out families. After the resumed bombing of the Sunday night, further canteens were brought into action on the Monday to meet the demands of the new homeless and the A.R.P. services. This was just one aspect of the sterling work done by the women of the W.V.S. and other welfare organisations during the blitz.

Amongst the many important Liverpool buildings which had 'got it' that Saturday night was the General Post Office, the saving of which was largely due to the devotion of its staff, for at a time when the Fire Service had more than it could possibly cope with on its hands, men and women post-office workers, who were officially off duty, flocked down to Victoria Street to help to fight the fire, which was still burning on Sunday morning. Many, clasping wet handkerchiefs over their faces, rushed into the building and struggled through smoke and flames to bring out valuable telegraph instruments. As a result of this wonderful and entirely spontaneous gesture on the part of its employees, the Liverpool Post Office saved virtually all its equipment, and a short time later was able to lend some of those same instruments to London when the capital found itself in need.

By the time night fell, an amazing amount of clearance, demolition and salvage had been accomplished, and all except seven of the fires were under control. The *Malakand* was among those which were still burning and every now and then the flash and roar of more bombs and shells exploding in her white-hot hulk rent the air. The ship took 74 hours to blow herself out.

Eleven o'clock came; 11-15; 11-30; 11-45; and still no sign of any raiders.

People began to believe it possible that they were going to have an undisturbed night. But, at a minute to midnight, their hopes were dashed by the moaning of the sirens, and for nearly four and a half hours the bombers showered thousands more incendiaries and hundreds of tons of high-explosives onto the wounded city.

That night the enemy planes flew to Merseyside in waves. At first only a few aircraft arrived, but thereafter, at five minute intervals, more and more bombers came upon the scene. They approached from all directions until at last the sky was filled with a sizeable fleet of them circling, albeit rather vaguely, over the area. A prompt, carefully-placed and intensive barrage of anti-aircraft fire kept the raiders at a considerable height and prevented any accurate target bombing.

A high-explosive fell on the Belgian Seamen's Lodging-House in Great George Square. The S.S. *Silver Sandal,* lying in mid-river, was hit, and St. Silvester's School was gutted. But the only well-known public building which was lost that night was the Rotunda Theatre in Scotland Road. The old Rotunda had already suffered one disastrous fire in 1877, but, restored, it had, during the succeeding sixty-four years, acquired quite a reputation as one of the leading provincial homes of melodrama. Across the years its boards had been trodden by many whose names glitter in the firmament of theatrical history - Dan Leno, Arthur Pinero, William Terriss and F.R. Benson, to instance but a few. On the night of May 4th, 1941, its long and glorious career reached its fiery end.

A little further north, Bootle was again attacked and, although its sufferings did not approach those of the previous night, a fair amount of house and industrial property was wrecked and a number of railway lines were put out of action.

It was about this time, too, that the late Ike Bradley, a noted Liverpool ex-boxer, was a near-casualty. Ike had forsaken the ring for a taxi driver's seat. He had just set down a fare and was standing near his taxi when a bomb fell. He was blown to the ground by the force of the explosion and his cab was destroyed. He, however, was unhurt. "Never even took a count," he afterwards grinned.

In all, seven enemy bombers were believed to have been destroyed in raids on Sunday night, six by fighters and one by A.A. fire. A grim token of enemy losses over the Merseyside area was the body of a Nazi airman, found floating in the Mersey on the Monday morning, who had, perhaps, fallen from the plane seen by air-raid wardens on duty in North Wales as it plunged in a sheet of flame.

Two lessons had emerged from the blitz so far; the value of the fire-watching schemes which saved at least a dozen of Liverpool's most famous buildings, and the efficiency of the Anderson shelters, to which many

Merseyside families owed their lives. The street shelters also had proved their worth. That Sunday night, when a square in the city received a direct hit, the nearby shelters, full of people, remained intact, except for some blast damage to the corners. There were, of course, the inevitable exceptions, and at one wrecked shelter under a school from which a number of bodies had been recovered, a soldier worked dementedly shifting piles of rubble with his bare hands, searching for his young wife whom he believed to be among those trapped there.

Perhaps that Sunday night was a mild one as compared with some of the other nights of the never-to-be-forgotten May Blitz, but, following on the holocaust of Saturday, it was quite bad enough, and when, at 4.23 a.m., the last of the raiders turned its nose towards Germany, the majority of Merseyside citizens were too tired to even care. For a while maybe the bombs would cease to fall, but that did not mean that they could rest. There was so much to do. So little time, it seemed, in which to do it. There were more fires to be fought, the dead to be buried, the living to be released from beneath the piled wreckage of homes and shelters, more streets to be cleared and unexploded bombs to be pinpointed and railed off. And now it was already Monday morning; in two or three hours time another week of work - much of it essential to the war effort - would be upon them. For the first time a momentary despair clutched at those wounded but still unbroken hearts. But a minute or two later it had been banished, and people were comforting one another with words like those which someone had scrawled upon a board which was perched unsteadily upon the summit of a mountain of broken masonry that had once been a church. "Trouble does not last always," it said.

5 GETTING IT AGAIN

Mr. & Mrs. Quayle sat in their parlour at "Seaview", Port St. Mary in the Isle of Man, and wondered how Mr. & Mrs. Smith, that nice couple from Liverpool who had always holidayed at their boarding-house in happier times, were getting on.

Seventy miles from Merseyside, the people of the Isle of Man could neither see nor hear anything of the Liverpool blitz, but they always knew when a raid was in progress because the island is linked with Liverpool by a stratum of rock and the impact of the heavy bombs would set the houses trembling and the windows rattling.

In the nearby internment camp at Port St. Mary, the internees also felt the tremors, and perhaps some of them rejoiced that the Luftwaffe was at it again.

At a military station near Hull, men of the King's Regiment listened helplessly to the deep-throated chugging of planes flying over the east coast en route for Merseyside, knowing that next morning a handful of little orange envelopes would flutter down onto the orderly-room table and send many of them speeding across country on compassionate leave.

Folk on the quiet green hills of Wales also heard the buzz and drone of aircraft, and later saw the black skies flower in flame.

And in the Isle of Man, in Yorkshire and in Wales they knew that the people of Liverpool were "getting it again."

And so indeed they were. For the fifth consecutive night, (Monday, May 5th) there were bombers over Merseyside.

Throughout the daylight hours of that Monday, all the work of tidying up after the Luftwaffe had been going on, and the inevitable crop of experiences swapped. The Bootle shopping queues were enlivened by the tale of the £4,000 in bonds and Bank of England notes which had showered down upon the houses and gardens of Hatfield Road.

Police and neighbours had collected those pennies from heaven and they were subsequently handed over to their legal owner. The explanation was that a portmanteau containing the bonds and cash had been taken into

an Anderson shelter with them by a man, his wife and daug
one Hatfield Road. A direct hit had wiped out the entire
portmanteau on which they were sitting was torn to shreds a
scattered to the winds. Inquiries were made in New Zealar
next-of-kin, but eventually a relative came from London
£4,000.

Monday morning was to bring further surprises for Mei

A Mr. L.L. Watson who was employed in an office in one (
buildings in the city had arrived there to find it had be
damaged. Thinking that it would be a good illustration of
defiant spirit if the national flag could be seen waving over
building, he promptly obtained permission to make the hazardo
the top of the dome and fixed three Union Jacks to the still servic
poles.

A tragic aftermath of Sunday's raids was the news of the de
film star, Mary Lawson, and her husband, Flight-Lieutenant
(Buster) Beaumont, when the house at which they were st
Liverpool was hit. Everyone else had gone to the shelter. Miss
gained fame at 17 when she succeeded Zelma O'Neal as 'Flo' in Go
at the Carlton Theatre, London. She had been in Liverpool in panton
before the war. Her husband was the elder son of La Dame de Sark.

It was on the Monday morning, too, that after that weekend of
special statement was addressed to the citizens of Liverpool by the Li
Civil Defence Emergency Committee, represented by the Lord
(Alderman Sir Sydney Jones), Alderman A.E. Shennan and Alderma
Hogan. It said:

"Liverpool has passed this, a very serious ordeal, during the la:
days and nights. We should like to take this early opportun
expressing to the citizens our great appreciation of the spirit in v
they have met the crisis."

The statement went on to express sympathy with the bereaved
those who had lost their homes and added:

"We wish to assure them that no efforts are being spared to see t
all the services which so vitally affect the city and the life of t
people at the present time are being maintained to the fullest possib
extent."

A further test was to come that very night.

It was just about five minutes past midnight when the sirens sounded
again, and fully four hours elapsed before the high continuous-noted
thanksgiving of the 'Raiders Past' was heard.

During those terror-filled hours thousands of the usual iron seeds of
fire fell from the overripe skies, and the Fire Service had to employ 80

23

of hosing, plus a considerable quantity of steel piping, in their efforts
m the resultant flowers of fire that sprang up all over the city.

The Bold Street-Berry Street area took a severe lambasting, and St.
s Church - the "Doctors' Church" as it used to be called - was
letely gutted. The nave and chancel were entirely destroyed, but the
walls and Foster's formidable tower remained standing. The bells,
ver, which had first sent their carillons out over Liverpool on St.
ge's Day 1829, crashed to the ground. Of all St. Luke's beautiful and
ric possessions, only the lectern, a couple of memorial chairs, a
orial desk and a bundle of altar cloths were salved.

Only an accident - some people might, and not without justice, call it a
cle - saved Liverpool Cathedral. A high-explosive bomb struck the south-
transept and pierced the roof. As it fell the bomb glanced the top of an
r brick wall which was supporting the central beam of the transept. That
impact was all that was needed to deflect the bomb outwards, and
nds later it exploded in the air above the street.

Had the bomb fallen in ever so slightly a different line, or struck the
l at an infinitesimally different angle, it would almost certainly have been
ected inwards to hurtle through the ceiling and cause havoc in the body
he cathedral. As it was, the blast destroyed many of the stained-glass
dows, including the large Derby Memorial Transept Window, which was
wn right out, the Golden and Sapphire windows and all those in the Lady-
apel. Another bomb, which actually fell on the cathedral steps, failed to
plode, but incendiaries which came down in the contractor's yard at the
st end of the cathedral started a large fire which did a fair amount of
mage to plant and equipment before the prevailing wind carried the flames
ross St. James's Road.

Windows were also shattered at Liverpool Town Hall, and the council-
amber was so badly knocked about that for a time it was unusable and the
ity Council had to hold their meetings in the Municipal Annexe.

The Duke Street building of the Liverpool Gas Company was gutted.
he Consumption Hospital in Mount Pleasant and the Royal Infirmary were
oth damaged by high-explosives. St. Silas's Church and a nurses' home in
Mulberry Street were hit. A high explosive bomb did serious damage to the
Emido flour-mills in Glasgow Street, where there was one fatal casualty. An
anti-aircraft shell fell and exploded in front of Fazakerley Hospital without
doing injury or damage, and two more fell in Everton Cemetery and the
playground of the Florence Melly School in Grandison Road, but did not
explode.

As usual Bootle came in for its share of the damage, with wrecked
dwellings, gutted warehouses and the now familiar, but none the less
pathetic streams of homeless ones. There were, however, fewer casualties in
Bootle, on this occasion and only two of them fatal.

Still on duty in the city when Tuesday morning dawned were three young fire-watchers - Miss Elizabeth Simons, aged 19, of Guest Street, Liverpool, Miss Kathleen Dowling, aged 20, of North Hill Street, Liverpool, and Mrs. Helen Watkins, aged 24, of Merlin Street, Liverpool - who had won the praise of all who saw them as they worked through the heat of the raids. Not only did these gallant girls put out fires, but they also managed to salvage a great deal of valuable material, including two cars.

Employed to look after a block of buildings in the Bold Street area, they put in a hectic weekend from the Friday night through to 6.50 on Tuesday morning. On the Friday night, at the height of the raid with bombs falling steadily, they had tackled a tool shop fire and brought it under control in five minutes. On the Saturday, Miss Dowling and Miss Simons had an amazing escape when they were sucked through a shop-window by the blast of a bomb and found themselves in a crater. Miss Simons was treated at hospital and was back at her post that night.

On the Monday, they had answered the call for volunteers from fire-watcher Mr. J. Gallagher, to enter a blazing school and recover property. Although a police-sergeant had warned them of the danger, the girls insisted on going in and succeeded in salvaging considerable property from the ground-floor.

Just twenty-four hours later, shortly before 12 o'clock on the night of Tuesday, May 6th, the enemy bombers were back in large numbers, and this time the brunt of the attack fell on Liverpool.

This sixth raid opened with the dropping of a heavy weight of high-explosives, followed by the inevitable spate of incendiaries. Throughout its four-hour duration, anti-aircraft defences fought a great duel with the marauding planes, but very soon the fires were springing to vivid life throughout the city. Most of them were quickly dealt with, but the Custom House, which had already suffered some eight months earlier, was set on fire and St. Catherine's Church in Abercromby Square, once associated with the Reverend Studdart Kennedy, famous World War I padre known to thousands of 'Tommies' as 'Woodbine Willie,' blazed so determinedly that the patients in the nearby Heart Hospital had to be evacuated with all possible speed at the very height of the blitz.

A. Mr. & Mrs. John Wilkes and their family had miraculous escapes when roof-debris crashed onto the shelter in the small yard at the back of the house in which they, Mrs. Wilkes's mother-in-law, Mrs. Hurley, and her daughters, the Misses Nora and Nellie Hurley, were sheltering. No one was hurt and, although the entrance was blocked, they all managed to crawl out through the emergency exit.

Later, Mr. Wilkes recovered from the wreckage of his home a battered bird-cage in which was the family's beloved canary, still very much alive.

Coopers' Building in Church Street was damaged. High-explosives fell in Moorfields, Seel Street, St. James's Street, St. George's Pier Head and on the Landing Stage. The Liverpool, London and Globe Insurance premises in Dale Street were heavily damaged by high-explosive bombs, and Bent's Brewery in Johnson Street was seriously fired. A service pipe-line at Dingle Jetty, and barges and two other vessels in Harrington Dock, were hit by incendiaries and high-explosives. West Toxteth Shed and Brunswick Dock Yard were extensively damaged. A police hut at North-East Brunswick Dock was demolished, and the constable on duty was so badly injured that he had to be taken to hospital.

A high-explosive which fell in the courtyard of Brunswick Gardens tenement flats killed six people and injured very many more. Some 50 high-explosives fell in the Mill Street district and five delayed action bombs in that area caused 1,000 people to be evacuated to rest centres and one main road to be closed. Liverpool casualty figures for that raid were 32 dead and 168 injured.

Several people were trapped in the cellar when a bomb dropped on the house in which were a Mr. & Mrs. Dodsworth and their daughters, Dorothy and Doreen. Their son and a young friend named Marshall were fire-watching at the time, and as the A.A. fire became very intense they went to the front-door of the house to look out. Hardly had they reached it, when the house was destroyed by a bomb. Marshall received a severe blow on the head, but he recovered quickly, and the two youths turned their attention to rescuing the people in the cellar. Working feverishly, they pulled debris away with their hands and, after a short time, succeeded in scraping a tunnel through which those who were buried wriggled to safety.

Again the firemen, both professional and auxiliary, were the heroes of the night, but matching their heroic courage is the story of Mary Halpin, a 19-year-old telephonist in the A.R.P. service. Whilst sitting at her telephone Miss Halpin had the nightmare experience of actually receiving the message that told of the destruction of her own home. She knew that her father, mother, four sisters and two brothers had been there, but she refused to leave her post, and it was not until she was relieved at the end of the raid that she joined her fiancé beside what remained of her home in Peach Street. There she found that her family had been rescued but, except for 11-year-old Teresa and 7-year-old Peter, both of whom had escaped with bruises and shock, they had all been taken to hospital.

Somehow, the slim tragic figure of Mary Halpin standing there beside her shattered home, her hands, face and uniform covered with the dust and dirt of six nights on duty, her tin hat tilted rakishly on the back of her head, becomes a symbol: the personification of all that was best in a Liverpool that steadfastly refused to bow its battered head.

6   THE SEVENTH SAVAGE NIGHT

The night of May 7th, which was undoubtedly the second most vicious of all the seven nights of the May Blitz, was also the last.

After a week of nightly raiding it seemed as though the ordeal would never come to an end, but it did, in the early hours of Thursday, May 8th, 1941. Merseyside had quite a few raids after that, but never again were they of anything like the severity of those which we were called upon to endure in that sorry spring.

The number of fires was not so great on May 7th as on the night of that worst-ever raid of May 3rd, but in some respects the situation confronting the fire services was decidedly worse, for throughout the week the state of roads, communications and water-supplies had steadily deteriorated. Moreover, the firemen themselves were, after six sleepless nights, practically out on their feet.

The alarm sounded at midnight, and once again the raiders approached in a number of distinct waves. Soon, a flickering curtain of flame stretched from Seaforth to Huskisson Dock and, under a merciless rain of bombs, the firemen worked frenziedly, their safety further imperilled by the threat of exploding shot and shell stored in quayside sheds and the packed holds of the ships whose masts and riggings made gaunt patterns against the red sky above the black dock-basins.

There were about 300 incidents in Liverpool and Bootle alone, whilst over the water considerable damge was done to property at New Brighton, and the Wallasey ferry-steamer, *Royal Daffodil II,* was sunk at her moorings at Seacombe Landing-Stage, seven of the crew who were on board at the time narrowly escaping injury. Until she was raised, in July 1942, the submerged vessel proved a severe hindrance to ferry traffic but, reconditioned, she afterwards returned to service in June 1943. Actually, the Mersey ferries played no small part in the battle against the bombers. Time and again the vessels were spattered with incendiaries and rocked by near misses, but never once did they fail in their task of maintaining the lines of communication between the Lancashire and Cheshire sides of the river. On one occasion during the May Blitz the Birkenhead ferry-boat, *Claughton,* had her saloon blasted by a bomb in mid-river, and later that same night another Birkenhead boat, *Bidston,* was severely damaged in her upper structure when pieces of massive concrete road-blocks were flung onto her deck as she lay at Liverpool Landing-Stage. Frequently, ferry employees carried out daring rescues of people who had fallen into the river, and on six occasions men of the Birkenhead Service received Liverpool Shipwreck and Humane Society awards for life-saving. the Birkenhead luggage boats, requisitioned by the Ministry of War Transport, also did yeoman service unloading aeroplanes and other deck-cargo from incoming freighters.

For Bootle that seventh night was the worst of the whole week. Street after street was flattened, and main highways, including Stanley Road, Rimrose Road and Southport Road, suffered major damage. Factories, warehouses, ship repairers, flour-mills, churches and timber-yards were fired and blasted. Among the victims of the cataclysm was Bootle's only theatre - the Metropole. The Metropole, where "Our Gracie" once played for £10 per week, where Florrie Forde, Gertie Gitana, Joe O'Gorman. Dorothy Ward and Shaun Glenville had all appeared in a blaze of glory, disappeared in a blaze of bomb-fire. Happily, no lives were lost, only a handful of ghosts died.

The most terrible single incident was the bombing of Stanley Road Co-operative Stores, where 50 people were trapped and killed in the subterranean shelter. A macabre touch of horror worthy of an Edgar Allan Poe was the blasting of Marsh Lane Mortuary. The Luftwaffe seemed determined that even the dead should not rest.

In Liverpool itself high-explosives fell on Tower Building and a provision warehouse in Sir Thomas Street. A curious thing, by the way, happened in Tower Building, where a bomb dropped straight down the light-well of the building, bursting at the bottom but doing little damage to the upper floors. There was extensive damage and fire in Atherton Street, and Hunter, Wilton and Clifford Streets were hit. Serious fires broke out in the Kensington district, and high-explosives, falling on a shelter in Bective Street, caused 11 casualties, 2 of which were fatal. Scotland Road, Great Nelson Street and Great Howard Street were heavily bombed, and a high-explosive demolished a shelter in Norris Street, causing 9 serious casualties.

Police-Sergeant F.W. Parrington, a noted swimmer and long-plunge champion, was among the victims of that last great raid. Sergeant Parrington held the plunging championship of the Amateur Swimming

Association eleven times between 1926 and 1939, and on September 30, 1933, he made the world record plunge of 88 feet 8 inches at Balliol Road Baths, Bootle.

Three elderly fire-watchers - 70-year-old George Thorne, of Clayford Crescent, Knotty Ash, 66-year-old Lewis Roberts, of Field Street, Liverpool, and 56-year-old Thomas Rimmer, of Tennyson Street, Liverpool - had to fight their way out of some shop property which was partially wrecked.

The men were together in one of the shops when the blast from a bomb which fell nearby ripped off a section of the building. "We were on the ground-floor of the shop," said Mr. Roberts, "when we heard the bomb whistle over the roof and crash with a tremendous roar. We dived for cover, and the next moment I was buried beneath ceilings and woodwork. I managed to fight my way out of the pile to see my mates in another part of the shop also getting free. I thought the end had come, and I was glad to escape with only a badly cut hand". Although severely shaken, all three decided: "We will carry on."

Quite a few shelters were damaged that night, too. Several bombs dropped close to a Liverpool church, near which a number of people were sheltering. One made a large crater in the churchyard, but the shelter withstood the blast and no one was injured.

Men, women and children were trapped in an underground shelter when the building collapsed on top of it, covering the entrance and emergency exits with tons of debris. Some of the shelterers were rescued alive during the night, and early the following morning rescue parties could still hear faint tappings coming from the wreckage. Soldiers and civilians on their way to work stopped to lend a hand to reach the trapped people.

At another shelter people had to be shepherded to safety by wardens because of a fire which had broken out.

The wonderful spirit exhibited by the shelterers on that and every night of the blitz was epitomised by the words and actions of Mrs. Marion Cousins, mother of sixteen children, and grandmother to another twenty-four!

She was among those who had to be hurriedly evacuated that Wednesday night from a menaced shelter. "When we began to feel the building falling on us, we realised we should have to get out quickly," she said coolly, and then she moved on to another shelter where, undaunted, she proceeded to lead some community singing.

At 4.30 a.m. on the morning of Thursday, May 8th, the sirens sounded the 'All Clear.' Merseyside's epic of endurance was over.

On all Merseyside more than 1,700 people had been killed, and another 1,154 seriously injured. Of the dead and wounded, the civil defence services had made up a relatively high proportion, with 28 wardens and members of the W.V.S. killed and 14 injured; 11 police killed and 51 injured; 27 casualty service workers killed and 6 injured; and 5 rescue men killed and 5 more seriously injured.

Those dark days had been illumined, too, by bright flashes of heroism. Heroism such as was displayed by a group of ten L.M.S. railwaymen who, heedlessly, took their lives into their hands when, on the night of May 3rd, an ammunition train in a siding at Clubmoor was set alight. A 34-year-old goods guard, George Roberts, was later awarded the George Medal in recognition of the leading part which he played in the affair. All along the train wagons were exploding, but the men calmly uncoupled the rear section before the flames had spread to it and shunted it out of danger. 34-year-old John Guinan, though officially off duty, rushed from his home in nearby Witton Road to the scene of the disaster, and continued uncoupling wagons despite repeated and violent explosions. Signalman Peter Stringer also displayed remarkable courage for, after being blown from his signal-box, he went grimly back to it to get on with the dangerous and complicated job of shunting.

Throughout the earlier part of May 8th the people of Merseyside prepared themselves for another raid. Automatically they went through all the motions of a routine that in the last week had become a part of their everyday lives. Rest centres were cleared in readiness for the next batch of raid orphans. Civil defence personnel were relieved and reinforcements took their places.

All the fire-fighting equipment which was not actually in use combating last night's fires was made ready to deal with the fresh outbreaks that darkness would surely bring. But that eighth mammoth raid never came. There was a warning, a few scattered incidents at Bootle, where houses and the gas-works were hit, but the fury of the Luftwaffe had exhausted itself.

By May 9th, between 6,000 and 7,000 workmen had been drafted into the area to clear the streets and make good the damage to factories and homes. By the end of the month, gas, electricity and water supplies were almost, if not quite, back to normal. Clearance of essential roads was virtually complete, and the railways, although still badly affected within the city, were handling a large volume of traffic. At the docks, where the Luftwaffe had done its worst, acres lay in smoking ruins, but their efficiency had been only temporarily impaired. The weekly figures of tonnages landed at the port speak eloquently enough for themselves:

Week ending:

May 3rd, 1941	145,596 tons
May 10th, 1941	35,026 tons
May 17th, 1941	85,678 tons
May 24th, 1941	84,032 tons
May 31st, 1941	93,283 tons
June 7th, 1941	108,773 tons
June 14th, 1941	126,936 tons

But there was still that other and very tragic side to the bright victory ... the sombre roll of Merseyside's dead. And on May 13th, 1941, Liverpool buried in a common grave in Anfield Cemetery 550 of those 'Unknown Warriors of the Battle of Britain' who never lived to see the fruits of that victory which their sacrifice had helped to bring about.

Their tomb was a tunnel of red brick, and the bodies - or bits of bodies - were interred in separate coffins, ranged two or three deep, and each covered with a Union Jack. Simple services were conducted from a dais above this vault by the leaders of the Liverpool churches, and there were scenes of pitiful grief among the mourners. The words of Dr. David, Bishop of Liverpool, brought aching lumps to the throats and stinging tears to the eyes of all present. "This piece of Anfield Cemetery," said the Bishop, "will always be held in honour as a specially sacred place. One day, no doubt, it will be marked by a monument enshrining the memory of the men and women and children of Liverpool who fell in a fight which, for them, was not a fight, for they sought not to kill but only to endure."

And the words which, later, Dr. Downey, the Roman Catholic Archbishop of Liverpool, used to describe the fury that was past, found their echo in many a heart.

"Liverpool," he said, "has been tried by fire, and I think I may say we have not been found wanting."

Indeed we had not.

Merseyside had matched its naked determination against the assembled might of airborne Germany.

And Merseyside had won.

7 BACKGROUND TO A BLITZ

In order properly to appreciate Merseyside's outstanding achievement in the face of its seven-night trial by fire, it is necessary to know something of the nine months preceding that catastrophic week – nine months during which the people of "a North-Western Port" learned by bitter experience the lessons which enabled them to carry on under a vicious bombardment.

For Merseyside the Battle of Britain began on the night of August 8th-9th, 1940, but prior to that there had been the wailing voice of the siren and the stomach-turning thuds of a few bombs. Actually, Merseyside's first alert was sounded on June 25th, 1940, and it was on that day, too, that the heavy double-noted throb that we were to come to know so well first droned from behind the low-hanging clouds. People ran to their dugouts and shelters. Civil defence personnel grabbed their tin hats and dashed to their action stations. Anti-aircraft crews took up watchful positions behind guns whose black mouth-gaps pointed hungrily at the sky. But... nothing happened. No bombs. No gunfire. The muttering of Goering's dark angels died away in the distance. The 'All Clear' sang out and, feeling perhaps a little foolish, everyone took up the threads of their normal lives where they had so abruptly dropped them.

It was during the following month that the bombs first dropped - three of them by a searchlight post at Altcar on the night of July 28th, and, about the same time, several more at Thurstaston, Irby and Neston. They fell in fields and did no particular damage, but the deep craters which they dug drew crowds of sightseers.

But it was as a string of six heavy bombs screamed earthwards at Prenton, Birkenhead, at 12.30 a.m. on that night of August 8th-9th, 1940, that Merseyside's battle really began with the spilling of the first blood.

The first of those bombs fell in the garden of the house of Captain Alan Layfield, commandant of the Special Police, who was on duty in Birkenhead Town Hall at the time. His wife and three other people had narrow escapes. The second bomb, however, scored a direct hit, striking the roof of Mr. & Mrs. W. Bunney's home, a few hundred yards away in Prenton Lane. In an upstairs room in that house a 34-year-old domestic servant lay asleep. She was killed instantly and passed into history as the first of Merseyside's 3,875 victims of the death that fell from the clouds. Her name was Johanna Mandale.

Within twenty-four hours of that first fatal bombing, a stick of seven high-explosives fell on Wallasey, spattering the black earth of a railway embankment, tumbling the bricks of houses at Stroud's Corner, Cliff Road and Mill Lane, and causing 32 casualties. And following close upon the heels of those first attacks on Birkenhead and Wallasey, there came, at midnight on August 17th, the first stick of bombs on Liverpool itself. Residents in the Caryl Street area heard the whistle of the bombs which fell in the Dock Road. The Overhead Railway and a corn silo were damaged, but the nearby tenements escaped. There was no loss of life and only six people were slightly injured.

On August 19th the first incendiary bombs to be dropped in Liverpool fell on the Eaton Road district of West Derby and at Norris Green. At one stage hundreds of them were burning but, fortunately, they mostly landed on open spaces. One, however, struck the Robert Davies Nursing Home, but did little damage.

There was a lull then until August 28th, when a series of spasmodic light attacks was initiated with the loosing of strings of incendiaries on Fulwood Park and Grassendale, and high-explosives on West Derby, Mossley Hill Church and Mersey Road.

In a small-scale raid on August 29th, the centre of the city escaped damage, but Bootle had its first attack and its first bomb - an incendiary - dropped on the gas-works in Hawthorne Road.

The third light raid, on the night of August 30th, saw incendiaries on the Dock Estate and Mill Road Infirmary, and high-explosives on Grafton Street and Brodie Avenue. That night, too, Wallasey High School for Girls was bombed.

On August 31st, however, the Luftwaffe stopped playing with us, and from that date until the end of November, Merseyside had almost continuous raids. The night of the 31st brought a heavy attack. In Liverpool alone there were more than 100 fires, mostly small, and the casualty figures were 23 dead and 86 injured.

In the city centre, Cleveland Square was badly knocked about, and the Custom House was hit and set on fire, while on the outskirts, houses were damaged in the Edge Lane area and fires were started at the Dingle Oil Jetty.

Bootle was again an important target, and at Wallasey the Town Hall was wrecked and its £3,500 organ absolutely destroyed.

September 1940, was in the main a month of what may be described as sharp raids. Out of a total of 20 raids Liverpool was bombed 16 times, Birkenhead 11 times, Bootle and Wallasey 9 times each, and Crosby 4 times.

The bombing of the Keilberg Children's Convalescent Home in Birkenhead on September 6th aroused widespread indignation, but happily there were no fatalities among its 30 little occupants. Nevertheless, people were angry. To bomb docks and factories, warehouses and power-stations was one thing, but these constant, indiscriminate attacks on hospitals, churches, schools and a score of other buildings which could not by the wildest stretch of imagination be construed as military objectives, were quite another matter. It got John Bull's goat and many of us sympathised with the emotion which impelled one man to chalk upon his window: "BEWARE HITLER, THERE WILL COME ANOTHER DAY."

On September 18th high-explosives fell on Walton Gaol, partially demolishing one wing and burying captives and captors alike. Twenty one bodies were taken away by the Mortuary Service. The Governor, however, was adamant that 22 of his prisoners were missing, and did everything short of accusing the service of aiding and abetting an escape. But the mortuary men stuck to their guns and the Governor was finally proved wrong when, eleven years later, the missing body was found beneath some rubble which was being removed from the blitzed wing of the prison.

September 26th was a baddish night with a substantial fire-raising raid on the docks that necessitated the calling in of fire-brigades from Bootle and Birkenhead. That night Birkenhead itself lost its world-famous Argyle Theatre, which was reduced to a mere shell. Other Birkenhead buildings seriously damaged included the Public Assistance Office and the Argyle Street Income Tax Offices.

An entry on the casualty sheet for the last day of September is especially poignant. Despite determined raiding by enemy forces, there was only one fatal casualty in Liverpool that night and beside the man's name was written the words "Caused by shrapnel."

October brought 15 light raids, in which the bombing figures stood at: Liverpool 14 times, Birkenhead 7, Bootle 6, Wallasey 3.

One of the most terrifying incidents of the entire month occurred on the evening of October 3rd. It was still daylight when a solitary, three-engined, German bomber suddenly swooped on a Liverpool bus. The bus was taking a number of women factory workers home when the conductor shouted to Driver H.O. Smith that a German plane was coming down low behind them. By then the aircraft was practically on their tail and Driver Smith could hear the rattle of its machine-guns. Quick as a flash, he accelerated and swerved to the opposite side of the road. One of the passengers, 17 year-old Lily Gilmore, who was on the upper deck of the bus with her friend, Joan Smith, afterwards described the chase. "We heard the plane first," she said, "and then we could see it clearly diving towards us. We heard a pinging noise and guessed it must be bullets spattering the roof. The driver of the bus went at a great speed and he did marvellously. He had us at a shelter in a very short time. The German plane was still machine-gunning as we raced for the shelter. There was an auxiliary fireman near and we saw his hat knocked off, presumably by a bullet. We saw the funny side of that later."

Though many of the October raids were relatively small affairs, their cumulative effect made a considerable impact on the life of Merseyside. But looking back we see them, and indeed all that went before, as a preparation: a preparation for November, the month in which Merseyside was to have its real baptism of fire.

8   THE HORROR NIGHT OF LAND-MINES

November 1940, will always be remembered as the month of the horror night of land-mines - November 28th.

These gigantic land-mines, which floated slowly down to earth below green parachutes, were something new, and at first no one knew quite what to make of them.

Indeed, one of the very first to fall caused a certain army sergeant no little embarrassment. This particular sergeant was an enthusiastic, but not especially popular member of his unit, and on the night in question he spotted what he thought was a German airman coming down by parachute. He immediately turned out the guard, and they charged with fixed bayonets.

Just then the moon came out from behind a cloud, and the soldiers saw the sinister shape of a giant land-mine swaying to and fro below its silken 'chute.

Never was the order to retreat given with such feeling or complied with more quickly. And never did an unpopular sergeant have more difficulty in living down an error of judgement.

One of the earliest of these land-mines came down on a mid-Victorian house in a residential quarter of Liverpool. It crashed through the roof and wall at an angle, its nose pointing bluntly into a bedroom. As it was the first unexploded mine ever to fall on the city, a high-ranking officer of the Civil Defence Service decided that he ought to go and have a look at it.

When he arrived at the house he found a naval rating with his ear pressed to the mine, and a young naval officer perched on the top of a rickety pair of steps coolly unscrewing the gain.

"I say, old boy, if this bally thing starts to tick you have precisely ten seconds before she pops," drawled the officer with a nonchalant smile.

"Thank you very much," said the visitor as he tiptoed out into the night!

The month opened in Liverpool with a series of nine lightish raids, which took place between the 1st and the 22nd. The first four raids were not very serious. A number of incendiaries dropped in Great Howard Street, the County Road area, on the East Lancashire Road and at Bowring Park, Huyton and Childwall. High-explosives fell on the junction of Queen's Drive and Townsend Avenue and in Wavertree Playground. The fifth, which lasted from 8 to 9.30 p.m. on the evening of November 12th, was the most violent. There were oil bombs on a post-office in Wavertree Road, high-explosives on Edge Hill Railway Goods Station, and severe damage was done to house property in Edinburgh, Saxony and Albert Edward roads. The death roll amounted to 13, and 18 people were injured. That was the night the B.B.C. came to Liverpool with one of its "They Went to It" programmes, and listeners all over the country heard the singing and chatter of 2,000 people in an underground shelter. Individual shelterers came to the microphone and told how bombs had wrecked their homes, and bus driver H.O. Smith was there to tell his story of the night the German bomber chased his bus. The Commandant of the Auxiliary Fire Service paid tribute to the permanent city fire-brigade, and A.R.P. workers spoke modestly of the work they were doing. The microphones went into the heart of dockland, and also to the Sailors' Home and the Gordon Smith Institute, where men of the mercantile marine service told cheerfully of hardships they had endured. And just to show the rest of the country that in spite of everything Merseyside was not a mournful place, the tour ended in a dance-hall where 1,400 dancers, ignoring the bursts of gunfire that drowned the drums, walzed and twirled under the coloured lights. The broadcast ended with a message from Liverpool to the capital, "If you can keep it up so can we." And London answered, "We can keep it up all right, and we are proud that you, Liverpool, are doing the same. So stick it, Merseyside, it's worth it."

The following night Wallasey had a raid in which considerable damage was done to corporation property in a number of places, but after that the borough enjoyed a five weeks' lull.

At 7.23 p.m. on the evening of November 28th, the sirens ushered in the 58th attack on Liverpool and, between that time and 4 a.m. the next morning, 150 planes unleashed all the fury of the Luftwaffe in the first really full-scale blitz on the port. This fearsome raid was the second major stroke in the air blockade which had been initiated by a medium-sized attack on Southampton five days previously.

In all the raids up to then Liverpool had suffered a total of 250 deaths. On that night alone, more than 200 people died. The main weight of the attack lasted two and a half hours until 10 o'clock, and hundreds of high-explosive and incendiary bombs, plus 30 huge land-mines (8 of which failed to explode) were unloaded upon the city.

Strangely enough, no incidents were reported from the city centre: that was the night when, in the language of the time, the suburbs "caught it." And catch it they certainly did - Allerton, Childwall, Wavertree and Woolton; Rose Hill, Edge Hill, Mossley Hill and Garston - despite a "ring of steel" put up by the anti-aircraft guns. Flares dropped by enemy planes made streets as bright as daylight. People in public shelters sang Christmas carols as the bombs whistled down. The blast from a high-explosive damaged one of the stands at the Stanley Greyhound Racing track, where the kennels were also hit. A number of dogs got loose, but only one was killed and the remainder were soon rounded up. In one house a grandfather-clock, which had been presented to its owner fifty years before, was stopped by a bomb for the first time in half a century. A man whose home was razed owed his life to the fact that that night he had gone to the cinema for the first time in two years. And then there was the Liverpool family that was trapped in a basement and was fed for twenty-four hours on milk which was poured to them down a long steel tube. Undaunted, they used this queer 'food-line' as a speaking-tube, shouting back messages of encouragement through it to those who were fighting to release them.

What Churchill afterwards described as "the worst single incident of the war" occurred that night when, at 0155 hours, a parachute land-mine demolished the Junior Technical School at Durning Road. There were close on 300 men, women and children taking refuge in a shelter in the basement of that building - people who normally used it, plus many more who had gone there four hours earlier when other shelters in the vicinity were damaged, and the passengers from two trams which had stopped outside it as the raid reached a climax. The land-mine brought the three stories of that solid building toppling down. The shelterers were trapped beneath the wreckage, and to add to the horror the school furnaces, which were situated in the basement, burst, and fire broke out in the debris. A heroine, whose courage must not be allowed to go unsung in any account of that awful disaster, was a middle-aged woman air-raid warden, Mrs. F.B. Taft. She it was who, half-choked by dust and the acrid fumes of smouldering woodwork, and with the level of the water from a burst boiler and a ruptured water-main slowly creeping up, did by her wonderful example prevent a panic. Here is what a husband and wife, two lucky ones who, miraculously, escaped that terrible carnage, had to say of her:

"If anyone deserves a medal it is that woman. She was magnificent in her courage and common-sense. Even as we heard groans from the dying, some of them children, she never cracked up. None of us thought that we would ever get out alive, but Mrs. Taft kept cheering up everyone. When people said, 'We'll never get through,' she just replied, 'They'll get us out all right.' A direct hit was made on the shelter just after my wife and myself had entered. The shelter lights fused, a boiler burst and a fire started at one end. The mass of people made it almost impossible to move about. The roof came through under the enormous weight of the debris and the best we could say was that we believed the victims' end was instantaneous. The horror of it all did not rob people of their courage. None of the women screamed. Nobody fainted. For the first few seconds we did not realise that we had been buried. We tried to scramble for the exits. Mrs. Taft said, 'Keep calm and try the emergency exits.' They were jammed, too. We all thought we were lost. Then, to add to our troubles, a fire started somewhere in he main section. I could see it over the brickwork. It wasn't apparently very large, but smoke poured into our part and people nearly choked with fumes. Water from the burst boiler and the broken water-main slowly flooded the floor of the shelter. It rose to our knees. We didn't know where it was coming from or where it would stop, and wondered if we should be drowned. Then Mrs. Taft shouted, 'I can see a light.' She had found a small window leading out of the shelter which had not been blocked by the terrific amount of debris. she raised a cry for volunteers to dig a way through. Four men came forward. They flashed a torch and someone outside saw it. Rescue work began." Mrs. Taft, her daughter and 3-year-old granddaughter were among those who escaped from the shelter. Doctors and nurses worked side by side with the firemen and rescue parties throughout the night. An auxiliary fireman told how he helped to extricate a little girl of about seven years old. She was trapped beneath two dead adults and could not move an inch. "While we were trying to get her out - and it took an hour or two," he said, "she was quite cheerful and seemed only concerned about her mother who was also trapped." The final casualty figures for Merseyside's most dreadful tragedy were: 164 killed and 96 injured. Between 20 and 30 people out of 290 escaped unharmed. A 24-year-old man was the last living person to be resurrected from that grim tomb. "We were amazed to see the man alive," said a rescue worker. "He had lived for two days in a pocket in the shelter formed by the debris. This pocket in the mass of the masonry had protected him from both fire and water. His first request to us was for a cigarette."

The half-dozen or so scattered bombs which fell in the vicinity of Edge Hill Station on the night of November 29th brought that sad month to a close.

During the past three months Merseyside had had a total of 44 raids, that is an average of one practically every other night. Now there was to be a welcome breathing-space of three weeks of relative peace before Hitler sent the Third Reich's Yuletide greetings to Merseyside.

9   HITLER'S CHRISTMAS GIFT TO MERSEYSIDE

Christmas was five days away. For three weeks there had been no raids on Liverpool. Men's minds had begun to turn cautiously to seasonal thoughts of peace and goodwill on earth. It could not, in the circumstances, be a merry Christmas. Was it too much to hope that it might be a quiet one? It was. Hitler had other ideas, and the three mid-winter nights of December 20th, 21st and 22nd, 1940, brought not gaiety but tears and sorrow to the Christmas hearths of 356 men, women and children who were to die during the week preceding the birthday of the Man of Peace.

The Führer's first Christmas gift to the people of the estuary was delivered by his Luftwaffe on the night of December 20th. The earliest messengers arrived at half-past six: the last of them departed at 4 a.m. the following morning. Parcels of incendiaries fell on the centre of the city, hitting the Town Hall, the Municipal Offices, the Central Police Offices, Prince's Parade, the Landing-Stage and the docks, and there was soon a fire situation so serious that reinforcements had to be called in from a wide area.

Fire broke out at Cunard Building and the Dock Board Offices, and food warehouses in Dublin Street and the Waterloo Grain House were set alight. The north wing of the Adelphi Hotel was badly blasted by a land-mine which dropped in Copperas Hill. About 200 bedrooms on one side were badly damaged, and the ballroom and grillroom also suffered. The decoration of the main court was also badly defaced, but no one in the hotel was killed, although one or two people were injured. Many of the guests were at dinner on the side furthest from the explosion. The lights went out, but there was no panic, and the hotel orchestra led the singing of *There'll Always be an England.*

A terrible thing happened in Bentinck Street when a series of five railway arches, beneath which many people had crowded for shelter, received a direct hit. Great blocks of concrete hurtled onto the packed ground, burying everybody. Rescue workers found themselves up against serious difficulties, because the concrete blocks were too heavy to move, and so tough that they turned the chisels of a number of compressors which were brought along to try and split them. When two days later, the clearance work was completed, 42 bodies had been recovered from that monumental pile of masonry.

Round about 6.30 on the evening of December 21st, Merseyside received the second instalment of Hitler's Christmas packets. This time the delivery took until 5 a.m. The raid was even more severe than that of the previous night, and involved a bigger force of raiders. Again, assistance had to be summoned to deal with incendiaries which fell on all parts of the city, and 30 police-officers were drafted in from the Lancashire County Constabulary.

The docks - particularly the northern sector - took a heavy hammering. City warehouses were hit. There were big fires in Hatton Garden, Hockenhall Alley and St. John's Fishmarket.

The market was absolutely crammed with poultry for sale for Christmas dinners and, as it burned, a delicious smell of roast turkey, goose and chicken drifted across the adjoining streets. Said one passer-by: "I've had a turkey on order there for some weeks, and I'm blowed if I'm not tempted to go in, bombs or no bombs, and collect it here and now."

Evans Sons, Lescher and Webb's chemical factory in Hanover Street went up like a giant firework, and fire also broke out at the electric power-station in Highfield Street, plunging the whole area into darkness.

St. George's Hall was struck by a shower of incendiaries and only the great vigilance of the Civil Defence, and the prompt action of the Fire Service, saved it. As it was, Willis's great organ, once one of the wonders of the modern world, had a narrow shave when an incendiary which had crashed through the roof was extinguished just as it was beginning to ignite it. Thanks to their protective wooden covering, not a single one of the 20,000 tiles of the hall's famous tessellated floor was so much as cracked. The two main assize courts were also untouched, but the sheriff's court, the chancery court and three other rooms were burned out. The Law Library was also destroyed by fire and, as Sir Harley Shawcross drily commented, "thousands of Law Reports contributed to the flames, more illuminating perhaps than they had ever been before!" Hundreds of people sheltering among the cells in the basement had no idea that the building was burning above them, but so much water was used in fighting the fire that the basement became flooded and they had to be evacuated.

The Royal Court Theatre narrowly escaped when a bomb fell in the roadway between it and the Victoria Hotel. Neither building was seriously damaged, but the bomb made a huge crater in Roe Street, into which a fire-engine which was responding to an urgent call was driven, and its entire crew of seven killed.

Mr. Malcolm Munro, of the Grafton Dance Hall, had his Christmas dance of Saturday, December 21st, ruined by the Luftwaffe.

"The people were just coming in at about 6.30 p.m. when the warning siren sounded," he said. "One of the first buildings to get a direct hit was the Olympia Theatre next door, and the blast took nearly half of the Grafton roof off. A hail of shrapnel scattered through the plaster ceiling and marked the floor right across, about two yards in front of the band stand. The musicians were in the alcove, but Mrs. Wilf Hamer, who was conducting, had to dive under the grand piano. We had about 200 dancers in, and they all stayed until the 'All Clear' at 5 a.m. The desolation in the West Derby Road district was indescribable. The electric tram wires were down, and the road was a positive sea of broken glass. On the Sunday afternoon we had arranged an audition for a young saxophone player from Derby, and we hastily procured tarpaulin sheets to cover the holes in he roof, and at 3 p.m. the audition took place. The young man got the job and later went to London. His name was Wally Stott. He is now one of the greatest orchestral arrangers for broadcasting and television bands."

Liverpool's best-loved church, the parish church of Our Lady and St. Nicholas, was among the victims of that brutal night. It was completely gutted, only the walls and tower were left standing. The fact that the tower was not destroyed was due to a stout oak door which kept the flames at bay until the fire-brigade could overcome them. When, eventually, the fire had been extinguished and the building had cooled down sufficiently to permit anyone to enter it, something very strange came to light. Those who went first into the ruined church found two charred beams which have since been set up in the porch of the new St. Nicholas's. Where the main altar had stood, someone - or *something* - had laid those two black rafters one upon the other in the shape of a cross.

The catalogue of that night's destruction seems endless. Severe damage was done to the Royal Infirmary, to Mill Road Infirmary and to St. Anthony's School in Newsham Street. A land-mine blasted houses on Queen's Drive, and one landed in Wyncote Road, Allerton. The Anfield district was especially badly affected, and a direct hit on a large shelter there provided the worst single event of the night, in which 74 people lost their lives. The raid spread to Bootle, Seaforth, Birkenhead and Wallasey, but none of those places suffered as badly as Liverpool.

On the third night - December 22nd - the raiders switched their attention to Manchester, but there was still some damage to docks and house property in the north end of Liverpool, and Birkenhead dockside warehouses were badly fired and blasted.

The following night saw some high-explosives fall into the river, and an unexploded anti-aircraft shell descended upon number 76 King's Drive.

There were no casualties or damage.

And that, for 1940, was that.

For the first time since its erection there were no crowds waiting below Russell Buildings in Church Street on New Year's Eve 1940 to see the little men with the hammers forge the first melodious music of the New Year. On the night of December 20th Russell Buildings and their quaint chiming clock had vanished in the flames.

The first two months of 1941 brought bad flying-weather, and although there were three raids in January and two in February, they paled into insignificance beside the Christmas blitz.

On the nights of March 12th, 13th and 14th, however, the Luftwaffe recovered much of its old fire. March 12th and 13th saw Wallasey's heaviest raids, in which 174 people perished and 432 were injured; 168 premises were totally destroyed, 366 had to be demolished, and 6,805 were damaged. Within less than two hours of the first attack, Wallasey's water-supplies for fire-fighting failed completely, owing to the trunk main having been broken by a bomb.

Birkenhead endured an eight-hour bombardment on March 12th, in the course of which 180 heavy bombs, 40 land-mines and numberless incendiaries were dropped. Half a dozen churches were damaged, and the presbytery of Our Lady's Roman Catholic Church in Price Street received a direct hit, killing Canon J.J. Tallon who had just returned from administering the last rites to people fatally injured during the raid.

In Bootle a man was holding the doorknob of the front-door of his house, which he was about to enter, when a bomb dropped further down the street. He was momentarily stunned, but otherwise unhurt, and when he recovered from the shock he found he was still holding the doorknob in his hand ... but the door had vanished!

In Liverpool itself there was considerable damage during those three days. Indeed, on March 12th it was only the southern districts which escaped. Fire destroyed the upper stories of the General Post Office and damaged the Municipal Annexe, the Cotton Exchange and the White Star Building. A land-mine came to ground in the university quadrangle, and another, which landed in Chatham Place, razed St. Anne's School. On March 14th about 200 incendiaries fell on Speke.

April was a kindly month with only three raids on Merseyside and a hearteningly light casualty list in spite of the number of unexploded land-mines which dropped.

But we must hark back to Sunday, March 16th, to recall one of the most curious incidents that ever took place in all blitzed Britain. That morning, a rescue party working amidst the rubble to which Wallasey's Lancaster Avenue had been reduced by the raid of March 12th, heard what sounded like the faint mew of a kitten coming from below the debris at their feet. They stopped work, leant on their picks and listened in silence. The mewing sound came again, but now they knew it was no kitten it was a baby's cry. Frantically, those three men tore at the stubborn bricks and clawed aside the earth, until at last they found the child. It was a little girl, a few months old, and she had lain buried there $3\frac{1}{2}$ days. But the will to live is a powerful thing, even when it resides only in the tiny body of a baby. They wiped the dust from the infant's mouth, removed a quantity of soft earth which was half choking her, and gave the little mite first-aid. As we used to say in those troublous times, her name can't have been on that bomb–thank God !

10 WHAT HAPPENED ON THE NIGHT

Broadly speaking, all the civil defence services fell into one or other of two groups. Either they were active services, such as wardens, police, fire, rescue and ambulance services, or else they were services whose work really began after the raid was over, such as rest centre, emergency feeding, billeting, demolition, clearance and mortuary services.

In considering the events of any one night, one is concerned primarily with the work of that army of active civil defence workers which took the field between the time when the City Electrical Engineer at Hatton Garden pulled down the lever that set off Liverpool's 49 sirens, and the time when, probably many hours later, he sounded the 'All Clear.'

The infantrymen of this great civilian army were the wardens and the police who, though they frequently proved themselves efficient and helpful Jacks-of-all-trades in an emergency, had the prime responsibility of acting as reporting agents. They were the people who had to make sure that every bomb that fell, that every incident that occurred - and the term 'incident' was a positive portmanteau of a word which was applied to anything from the death of a solitary cow in a field to the blowing up of a graveyard full of corpses - within their area was reported to divisional sub-control.

In addition to their normal duties of taking care of the public and attending to the problems of traffic control, the police also took charge as 'incident officers,' setting up an incident post at the scene of every major disaster. This incident post then became the focal point from which messages were despatched and the operations of all the various services called to deal with the emergency were co-ordinated.

At the outbreak of war there were 2,560 whole-time, paid wardens, and a further 15,740 part-time, volunteer wardens in Liverpool. The Warden

Service came, technically, under the authority of the Chief Constable, but the main burden of organisation was taken off his shoulders by Major James Bennett, Liverpool's Chief Warden. As with the other civil defence services, the wardens' organisation was based on the police divisions of the city, and each division was commanded by its divisional warden. These divisions were all broken up into groups: there were 41 of them, and the groups were further divided into sectors, of which there were 748. A sector post served every one of these sectors, and it was from that post that all sector operations were directed. Some of those posts were specially constructed: some were attached to air-raid shelters: others were established in existing premises, carefully protected and strengthened with sandbags. In addition to their function as reporting agents, the wardens had wide duties as local guardians of the people. These included keeping an eye on the shelters and their occupants, getting to know local residents and their habits, so as to know where to search for them in the event of their houses being hit, shepherding people to rest centres, enforcing blackout restrictions and assisting the police to evacuate houses and cordon off after the fall of unexploded bombs. Many women found their place in the Warden Service and were invaluable in supplying little extra feminine touches of comfort.

Both wardens and police received considerable assistance in their work as reporting agents from the Civil Defence Messenger Service. In 1940 Professor Channon of the university had organised a Liverpool Civil Defence Cadet Corps. It was made up of youths in their teens, and this corps, augmented by 100 motor-cyclists and 250 pedal-cyclists (including a number of Boy Scouts) who had volunteered to serve on a part-time basis, became the Messenger Service. Later on, in the May Blitz, when all the telephones were out of commission, this service became very important and did some exceedingly good work.

Of all the services, that which had the heaviest burden to bear was undoubtedly the Fire Service, and at no time did it show up to better advantage than during the May Blitz. On the night of May 3rd no fewer than 400 fires were attended, and the Fire-Brigades Regional Reinforcement Scheme had to be called into action. Assistance from upwards of 130 outside brigades was enlisted, and during the next few days it became a familiar sight to see engines bearing the names of many different towns on their scarlet sides lined up in the road outside the Central Fire Station in Hatton Garden. During the raid on the night of May 3rd-4th, a 14-inch water-main supplying a large portion of the city's shopping centre was fractured, causing the disastrous shortage of water which led to the burning of Blackler's. Between the 5th and 8th May, lengths of 6-inch steel piping were laid along five different routes from Salthouse Dock, the Landing-Stage, Stanley Park Lake, and Bramley Moore and Canada docks to ensure adequate additional water-supplies. Thus it may be said that the Mersey itself played no small part in fighting for Liverpool, and powerful pumps at Nova Scotia were employed to replenish the salt-water main from the river. When, on the night of May 3rd, there was a breakdown in telephone communications, the control of the Fire Service was immediately switched to Allerton Fire Station, and the outriders of the Messenger Service covered themselves with glory. During that one week of the May Blitz, 18 firemen were killed and 162 others were injured.

That Merseyside did not suffer even more seriously from fire than it did, was due in no small measure also to the united efforts of a large body of fireguards, street fire-fighters and fire-watchers.

Early in 1941 the Chief Warden had received instructions from the Emergency Committee to organise street fire-fighters and train them in the use of that faintly Heath-Robinson contraption, the stirrup-pump. By the time the May Blitz began, 53,109 persons, formed into 6,226 fire parties, equipped with 6,191 stirrup-pumps, were mobilised to cope with the fire from the sky. In the course of Liverpool's blitz many valuable properties were saved by the prompt action of the Fire Guard - among them the Cunard Building, the Liver Building, Martins Bank Building, Derby House, the Town Hall and St. George's Building in Lime Street, where the late Alderman Luke Hogan, emerging no doubt from the sacred preserves of the Press Club, distinguished himself by dealing with several incendiaries on the roof.

In addition to the 50,000 street fire-fighters, a further 50,000 citizens undertook fire-watching duties at their places of employment, and 16,000 performed fire-guard duty on rota at 10 dormitory depots which were set up. These depots accommodated up to 200 personnel per night.

Fifty-two fire huts were erected in various parts of the city for training purposes, and a school for instructors was opened in Norton Street. Altogether more than 105,000 fire-guards were trained, excluding 4,000 who were taught by the National Fire Service to man 136 trailer pumps which were sited at strategic points all over Liverpool.

The Fire Prevention (Compulsory Enrolment) Order of 1941 provided that all men between the ages of 18 and 63 should register for duty, and 120,000 citizens duly registered. All save 1,500 or 1,600 of these were exempt, however, for various reasons.

Some little time invariably elapsed between the date of registration and the call to duty, and in one case a man who had been ordered by letter to present himself, replied from El Alamein that he would be delighted to do so providing transport home was laid on! Another reply, couched in somewhat grimmer terms, read: "Am writing on behalf of Mr.___ who is unable to report for duty as he is now fire-watching for a higher authority. He died last Tuesday."

Towards the end of the war, the Government introduced compulsory fire-watching for women. Although many hundreds of women had already volunteered, and government departments had for some time required their female staff to undertake such duties at post offices and in other government premises, this order aroused a good deal of bitter feeling. In Liverpool, the Emergency Committee saw to it that the order was complied with only in the very gentlest way. No woman was ever required to do duty in warehouses or any places which were deemed unsuitable, and women were used in the main to fill in during the short periods of daylight on summer evenings and on Saturday and Sunday afternoons.

And so, in any final assessment of the way in which Liverpool defied the flames, John - and Joan - Citizen must take an honoured place beside the ranks of gallant firement who, heavy-eyed, with smoke-blackened faces and boots that squelched ice-cold water at every step, fought for many days and seven sleepless nights to save their city from the fury of the fire.

11 AFTERMATH OF A RAID

When we think of air-raid casualties we generally think in terms of the wounded and the dead. Those were, it is true, the most dramatic and the most terrible sorts of casualty, but there were other scarcely less pathetic casualties in the form of thousands of people - most of them pitifully poor - who suddenly found themselves homeless - bewildered orphans of the air-raids.

The authorities, having read the reports of the Spanish Civil War and refreshed their memories with confidential summaries of the aftermath of more recent German bombing raids on the Low Countries, were alive to the fact that the post-raid care of the civilian population constituted a major problem of modern warfare.

The first official pronouncement on this complicated subject was ERIK - a circular outlining the principles of emergency relief in kind - the upshot of which was that the various public assistance departments were to be charged with this work, and the first thing that Mr. G.W. Molyneux, the Chief Public Assistance Officer, did was to set about establishing a number of rest centres.

Typically, a rest centre was a church or mission hall with only very limited facilities. It was stocked up with supplies of blankets and mattresses, and a number of locked steel ballot-boxes, of a type that had been used as shell boxes in the Boer War, containing iron rations. Between 150 and 200 halls were thus frugally equipped, and 60 large mansions were as casually converted into hostels for the reception of families who were, for one reason or another, likely to be difficult to billet.

The staffing of the rest centres was undertaken by members of the Women's Voluntary Service, together with housewives from the surrounding district.

Obviously, the rest centre was essentially only a very temporary refuge - a street with a roof on, you might call it - which was designed to operate on a twenty-four hour basis. The weeping victims of the bombs would be shepherded there by police and wardens, and there they would find kind words and - perhaps most important of all - a nice hot cup of tea, as strong and as sweet as rationing would allow. Later, a light meal would be served. This first meal was the responsibility of the Public Assistance Officer, and was usually cooked in the large kitchens of one or other of three city hospitals. It was then transported to the rest centres by the Rest Centre Service's own transport fleet. All further catering was carried out by the Emergency Feeding Service. This service had been established under the Director of Education, Mr. C.F. Mott, and he, as Emergency Feeding Officer, was in charge of all its operations. On the outbreak of war the cooking facilities of the School Meals Service had been adapted to meet the needs of an emergency service for the city. Generally speaking, the plan worked smoothly, but the May Blitz produced a very awkward situation. Bomb damage had reduced the catering services on the docks to nil. The port had to be kept working, and if the dockers were also to be kept working they had to be fed. At that time the Emergency Feeding Service consisted of the Education Committee's Central Kitchen at Green Lane, Stoneycroft, four 'shadow kitchens' at school premises, four Ministry of Food Cooking Depots, two British Restaurants, preparing and serving breakfast, dinner and tea, and four British Restaurant Canteens, serving only midday meals, and a very great strain was put upon its resources. The Central Kitchen in Green Lane became the focal point of the scheme, and a staff of 65, working there day and night on a three-shift system, managed to supply daily, on four days of the attack, 16,000 hot dinners to dockers, members of the A.F.S., first-aid, rescue and ambulance services, as well as to employees of private firms engaged on war work, and a host of school children. The huge quantities of food-stuffs required daily for these meals included 3,000 lbs. of meat, 70 cwt. of potatoes, 20 cwt. of turnips, 20 cwt. of carrots, 300 gallons of milk, 1.1/2 cwt. of sugar and 72 lbs. of margarine. The total number of meals supplied at all emergency centres throughout the May Blitz was 79,510.

Relief gifts of many kinds flowed into the stricken city from the Empire and the U.S.A. They included a number of mobile canteens, bearing the crests of the various Dominions on their sides, which were allocated to the Public Assistance Committee and proved of very great help. Thousands of parcels of clothing were also received from the British War Relief Society. These were directed to the city's several clothing relief stores. On one occasion Mr. Winthrop Aldrich, subsequently the American Ambassador and at that time President of the War Relief Society, visited Liverpool, and in the course of a luncheon at the Town Hall suddenly expressed a desire to inspect one of the emergency relief stores. Whilst walking around the store he was told that it was often necessary to completely reclothe people who had been bombed out, and that this particular store could do just that.

"Then give me a back collar-stud," said Mr. Aldrich.

It was handed to him in a matter of seconds.

"My! That's wonderful," exclaimed the V.I.P.

He never knew how desperately a stores assistant had struggled behind some close-packed shelving to tear off his collar and hand the visitor ... his own collar-stud!

Fed, clothed and provided with small sums of money by the Assistance Board, the next problem was to find accommodation of a more permanent nature than could be managed in the rest centres for Merseyside's homeless.

This formidable task was the responsibility of Mr. George Binns, the Chief Building Officer.

The story of billeting in Liverpool is essentially a story of one man, forty women and a team of sanitary inspectors. The women were school-teachers, ex-nurses, clerks and a nun, who, feeling the need to assist in the emergency, had received a dispensation from her order. They were indeed a motley collection. There was 'Mac,' who, a couple of years before, had been a medical student in Durham, and now rejoiced in the title of 'Officer Commanding Beds'; there was 'Hilly,' who could find homes for families ranging from three to twelve almost before you could blink an eye; there was 'Hickey,' who walked amidst the debris of devastation with seraphic calm and a saint-like smile; and there was 'Wattie,' a young man without any previous administrative experience who had been brought from the R.A.F. because of the brilliance of the original scheme which he had propounded during the early days of the phoney war.

The fantastic efficiency of the Billeting Service was largely due to the fact that, during the summer of 1940, before the air-raids had begun, a tremendous house-to-house survey had been carried out by the sanitary inspectors, and a vast card-index of all available billets compiled. The organisation behind all this was absolutely first-rate, and, indeed, Mr. Binns not only acquired a national reputation as a result of his work, but was generally regarded as the foremost man in the country so far as billeting was concerned.

On the morning following a raid, the billeting officers would appear at the rest centres, their indexes under their arms, and by nightfall the centre would be clear and ready for the reception of its next flock of refugees. It was the service's proudest boast that seldom did anyone have to remain a second night in a rest centre, even during the crisis of the May Blitz when some 41,005 people were found billets within the city in the course of one week.

But billeting was only a temporary measure. Sooner or later the question of rehousing had to be answered. All houses becoming vacant on the corporation's own estates were reserved for blitzed families; privately-owned unoccupied houses were requisitioned on an extensive scale, and quantities of essential furniture were supplied by the local authority, but even so accommodation fell terribly short of what was required, and with billets crammed to capacity and every possible house requisitioned, 9,852 people had to be evacuated to reception towns and areas outside the city.

Certainly, those were not pleasant days, but in remembering them one is warmed by the recollected glow of that wonderful spirit of comradeship and lending-a-helping-hand which was abroad amid the ruins. What a pity that it should take the greatest war the world has ever seen just to make people be kind to one another.

12   CLEARING UP THE MESS

The 'All Clear' has sounded. The living emerge from shelter and cellar. Grandfather clambers out of his earthy Anderson: father crawls from under the kitchen table. The dead and wounded are carried from out the wreckage. Another raid is over. But for those whose job it is to clear up the mess, to restore disrupted services and repair damaged property, the work is just about to begin.

In this gigantic task of sweeping up after the Luftwaffe, one of the heaviest burdens of responsibility fell upon the shoulders of a section of the civil defence services organised, operated and controlled by Mr. Herbert Hamer, Liverpool's then City Engineer and Surveyor - the Debris Clearance and Road Repair Service.

This was obviously work of prime importance, for blocked roads meant far more than the mere disorganisation of transport; they meant that the efficiency of fire and ambulance services was disastrously impaired. The Debris Clearance and Road Repair Service also undertook the erection of barricades and notices to close roads which had become unsafe because of dangerous buildings, fires or unexploded bombs.

Although prior to the May Blitz this service had had quite a bit of practice in the work which it was required to do, during that week of May 1st-7th the damage was on so huge a scale that the 200 or so manual workers available could not possibly hope to be able to cope with it.

Approximately 500 highways, including the majority of Liverpool's main roads, were closed, and some could not be reopened for several weeks until dangerous buildings had either been demolished or else made safe. Some idea of the extent of the damage may be gained from the fact that it was estimated that the total cost of repairing the city's streets would be £200,000 in respect of damage directly due to enemy action, whilst a further £50,000 would be added to the bill by damage done to the footways during subsequent side-clearance. Strange as it may seem, there were remarkably few instances of bomb craters actually in the roadways, and only one road bridge, that in Stanley Road, near Melrose Road, was irreparably damaged. In central areas, however, soft wood block surfaces suffered badly, and in Deane Street the surface of the granite sett paving was shattered by the intense heat of blazing buildings on either side of the street.

By May 7th, however, a pool of 6,000 men had been formed at the City Engineer's main workshops at Breckside Park, and work started on the formidable business of clearance. This labour pool was made up of 3,000 members of the Armed Forces, 2,000 men employed by civil engineering contractors in the Merseyside and Manchester areas, and a further 1,000 men who, temporarily out of work as a result of the blitz, had been sent up from the city's labour exchanges. It soon became apparent that to transport debris from the city centre to established tips on the outskirts was quite impracticable, and temporary tips were erected on vacant sites in Byrom Street, Pitt Street and Netherfield Road.

Practically every tramcar route was seriously affected, and on May 4th only 13 per cent. of the total route mileage was in use. All bus services were, however, maintained, diversions being made where necessary.

Quite apart from blockages due to falls of debris, tramway services were also disrupted by the auxiliary water-mains which, after the failure of water-supplies for firefighting on the night of May 3rd, had been laid along and across a number of roads. Normal wheeled traffic was carried over the pipes by timber ramps, but it was not until later, when the Home Office consented to the burying of the mains at road crossings, that the trams could run again.

The whole question of water was an anxious one, and the Waterworks Emergency Organisation was kept at a peak of activity throughout the May Blitz. Water-mains were affected by 340 incidents, requiring 700 repairs, many of which involved re-laying up to 50 yards of main. The department's main workshops in Pall Mall were fired by incendiaries and a large amount of repair equipment was destroyed. Three service reservoirs, at High Park Street, Kensington and Breeze Hill, were damaged but, fortunately, all three were able to remain in commission after the water-levels had been regulated. The operation of control valves on fractured mains, in order to prevent continuous waste and possible flooding, temporarily deprived certain areas of their water-supply, but fleets of water-wagons, together with three carts loaned by Messrs. Reece, remedied the deficiency to the tune of 91,000 gallons a day. Between the 1st and 7th of May an extra demand of more than 70 million gallons of water was imposed on the waterworks storage reservoirs through enemy action.

Those responsible for other public utilities, such as gas and electricity, also found that the 'All Clear' acted for them as a summons to work.

The Liverpool Gas Company sustained breakages of more than 500 gas-mains during the May Blitz, and its employees, assisted by workers from gas undertakings and the Pioneer Corps, were kept pretty busy supplying over 120 square miles of the company's area with the required amount of gas. During the height of the blitz the company lost its Duke Street building, where the control room was situated, and it was only with considerable difficulty that the mains' records and control equipment were salvaged.

Damage to gas and water mains situated in the same crater often resulted in the gas-mains becoming flooded. On one occasion a bomb landed outside a dairy which was situated on rising ground off Prescot Road. Thousands of milk bottles which were on some lorries at the dairy were smashed, and the milk flowed downhill into the crater where, mixed with the water from the broken water-mains, it flooded the gas-mains. At breakfast time the following morning scores of housewives in the lower reaches of Prescot Road could not believe their eyes when they turned on the gas and milk came out!

The Electric supply Department also had its troubles during that savage week of May. Thirty-four sub-stations were destroyed or damaged, and underground cables were damaged at 705 points. But, thanks to excellent work in the way of temporary repairs, Liverpool was not seriously inconvenienced. Clarence Dock Power-Station, which was straddled with high-explosives and hit by incendiaries, and Lister Drive Power-Station, which was blasted by a land-mine, both received damage, but it was not of a very grievous nature. The most spectacular incident was the lifting of an 8 horse-power van over the 22 foot wall of the Paradise Street Sub-Station. The van fell through the roof and came to rest wedged between two rotary converters.

And on top of all this work of immediate priority there was the slower, less vital, but still very necessary work of salvage and of house repair.

So, as the sirens sound the 'Raiders Past' and the majority of citizens hurry off to snatch a few hours sleep before the dawn of a new day, we may picture the work of restoration starting. Out into the darkness of a blacked-out city slip the men with a purpose. The men of the Debris Clearance and Road Repair Service who will, between now and the next raid, shift thousands of tons of a tumbled city; the men of the Demolition Squads, who will push and pull the last remnants of perilously tottering buildings to the ground; the water-engineers, the gas-men, the electricians, the post-office engineers who will give the voices back to dead telephones. The night has grown chill, but the firemen are sweating as they play their hoses on hundreds of fires. The ambulances are purring through the darkness carrying their tragic cargoes

13 SHELTERS AND SHELTER LIFE

No story of the Great Merseyside Blitz would be complete without its chapter on shelters and the weird cave-dweller sort of life which thousands of people lived in them.

The need for air-raid shelters had been recognised well before the actual declaration of war, and when on that fateful morning of September 3rd, 1939, Mr. Chamberlain announced in a sad tired voice that we must now consider that a state of war existed between Great Britain and Germany, Liverpool had already sufficient public shelters prepared for the accommodation of 33,750 persons, and a further 180,650 people had been provided with domestic shelters.

By May 1940, those figures had increased to:

Public Shelters - 55,585 persons. Domestic shelters - 366,731 persons.

And finally, by May 1944, the peak figure of:

Public shelters - 80,204 persons. Domestic shelters - 700,510 persons, had been reached.

During those first months of the phoney war the shelters stood empty. People began to talk of their being a waste of money. "We'll never need them," they said. "It'll all be over by Christmas." But after the first raids of 1940 there was no more of that sort of talk and the air-raid shelters did not lack tenants. Indeed, those shelters had now begun to provide something more than a mere refuge; they had gradually developed into popular social rendezvous, where large groups of citizens could gather together to find comfort as well as safety in numbers.

Night after night, as dusk fell, the trek to the shelters began. Pathetic streams of women and children, looking, with their bundles of bedding and bags of food, like so many refugees, wended their way to the shelters. And there they settled down in their usual spots and set about preparing meals for the men-folk who would come 'home' to the shelter direct from work.

As time wore on shelter life became quite a highly-organised affair. The larger shelters acquired canteens or running buffets. Sick-bays were initiated, and isolation sections, staffed by trained nurses, were provided for children taken ill with infectious diseases. And as the raids became more frequent, people began to live an ever increasing part of their lives in the shelters - eating, sleeping and getting to know one another there. Babies were born, birthday parties were held, card schools were formed. There were the quiet readers and the solemn chess players, and there were also the jolly ones with their singsongs and their accordions. Liverpool had gone to ground and was making the best of it. In many of the public shelters quite a family atmosphere developed among the regulars. Every family had its own special place and there was considerable discontent if strangers, all unconsciously, usurped their particular plot!

Many of those who came regularly to the public shelters had in fact been provided with domestic shelters, and official efforts were made to persuade all families who were not genuinely homeless to return to their own homes. At each of the larger shelters a register was compiled of the names and addresses of all those who used the shelter regularly, and their homes were visited to check on whether their houses were habitable and if alternative shelter facilities were provided either in the house or somewhere nearby. If this proved to be the case, such people were politely told that they must not use the large public shelters. So, gradually, the numbers were reduced to proportions which could be organised and properly catered for.

A high proportion of those who came to the shelters in the central areas were not residents in the immediate vicinity. Some were people living in the suburbs who, impelled by some peculiar fear, felt that they must travel into the heart of the city to go to a particular shelter. There was, for instance, one gentleman of considerable wealth who always insisted upon coming to a public shelter in Deane Street because his wife was convinced, and had convinced him , that it was the safest place in the entire city! Actually, it was probably one of the most dangerous, because it was situated below the pavement lights. Another lady made a nightly journey from the quiet byways of the Wirral to Liverpool in order to occupy the darkest and dampest corner of a basement shelter in Mathew Street, explaining that her intuition informed her that this was the spot she must choose!

Of course the conduct and care of all these people who were being forced to lead such utterly unnatural lives presented the authorities with some knotty problems. There was, for example, the problem of the bedding. Some shelterers decided to leave their blankets and mattresses in the shelter rather than lug them there every evening. The trouble was that many of them became infested with vermin. In view of such conditions, the Emergency Committee decided to appoint an Air-Raid Shelter Inspection Department, composed of sanitary inspectors from the Corporation Public Health Department, and to be known as the Shelter Welfare Service.

A comprehensive survey of all public shelters was immediately undertaken, and there were many installations of such essential items as water-borne sanitation, hot and cold water, heating apparatus, cooking facilities and bunking.

All these improvements came about as a result of the work of the sanitary inspectors, who visited the shelters continuously day and night, seven days a week. It is only fitting that a tribute should also be paid to the drivers of the cars which carried the shelter inspectors from shelter to shelter, often through very bad patches of bombing.

In addition to their duties as guardians of public health, the sanitary inspectors also became sentinels of public morals, and their shelter welfare work included keeping a sharp eye open to see that the abnormal conditions of communal life did not lead to any improprieties.

The larger shelters, providing the basic problems, were situated mainly in the central areas of Liverpool. They were vast refuges accommodating as many as 1,000 persons, and great care had to be taken by officials not to transmit any information likely to cause a panic. On the whole, the behaviour of the shelterers was exemplary, but on one occasion, due to the damaging of St. George's Hall, the crowds who normally took refuge in its basement besieged James Street Low Level Railway Station and forced an entry. An attempt was made to keep the people out, but eventually it was realised that it would have to be accepted as a public air-raid shelter. Adequate sanitation was laid on, the platforms were marked off for bunking, and it, together with Central Low Level Station, became Liverpool's equivalent to the London tubes.

Following this victory of the public will, there were urgent representations from certain quarters that the Mersey Tunnel ought to be turned at night into a kind of gigantic shelter. A wise authority remained obdurate, however, in its refusal to do anything of the sort. This would have been a very bad plan, for not only would it have meant impossible crowding at the exits and entrances every time the sirens sounded, and a calamity of unthinkable magnitude had, by some mischance, the tunnel been breached, but it would also have meant that fire-engines and ambulances could not have been brought swiftly from one side of the river to the other. The way had also to be kept clear to enable naval land-mine disposal teams to be brought from Chester to Liverpool as quickly as possible.

And then there was 'Mr. Mitchell' to consider.

'Mr. Mitchell' was a smoke-screen unit, which produced a most horrible smell and great clouds of foul thick smoke, used by the military to set up a protective screen on clear nights, and he was always being trundled through the tunnel.

Liverpool's shelters, in most cases, stood up wonderfully to the bombardment. Here and there, there were terrible tragedies as the result of direct hits but, glancing through piles of photographs, one notices time and again that amidst a levelled landscape of spilled bricks and tumbled houses, the shelters still stood.

Occasionally shelters were put to other and less worthy uses than those for which they were intended. Thus, a court case of the time reveals that at least one, on the Dock Estate, did service as a hideaway for stolen property!

Towards the end of the ordeal many shelterers, grown tired of the incessant roaring of the bombs and grumbling of the guns, piled into bread vans, lorries and any other transport that could be pressed into service to take them out to such places as Maghull and Huyton Woods for a quiet night's rest in barns, outhouses, fields and hedgerows. It seems odd to think that to-day many of those who trekked nightly from the stricken slums to the country are now living in ultra-modern corporation houses on the very sites where once they camped in ditches. But it is strangest of all to look back to the time when the dogs of war drove men and women back to the cave life out of which they had emerged all of 5,000 years before.

14   END OF A HOLOCAUST

An observer looking back across the years at the Great Merseyside Blitz as a whole, might interpret it in terms of a symphony - a symphony of battle.

Its first movements were slow and muted, with only an occasional loud passage to hint at the terrific crescendo which it was to reach in May 1941. Thereafter, the echoes died away and the martial music of guns and bombs ended in a long silence which lasted from 1942 until the end of the war. Never again after that fearful night of May 7th, 1941, were Merseysiders called upon to withstand the full weight of a really heavy attack from the air.

After Thursday, May 8th's, ineffectual raid there were to be only eight more attacks on Liverpool, most of which were of a very light character.

From 12.51 a.m. on the night of May 29th until 3.53 a.m. the following morning, there were bombers over Merseyside. Eight dwelling-houses in Beaumont Street were seriously damaged by high-explosives. Five bombs fell in a wheatfield on Croxteth Estate. Others fell in fields skirting Mab Lane, West Derby, and the orderly room of the R.A.S.C. depot in Deysbrook Lane was demolished. But the casualty list showed only one fatality and three people seriously injured.

On May 31st there was another raid, from 1 a.m. to 3.30 a.m., with incendiaries on West Coburg, North-West Toxteth and Brunswick Docks. A high-explosive damaged a water-main and an electric cable, and blew out the windows of houses in Stanley Park Avenue, and two houses in Townsend Avenue, which had been previously damaged and evacuated, were demolished. There were no casualties.

The following night, June 1st, brought a somewhat larger fleet of enemy planes to Merseyside, but an exceptionally intensive A.A. barrage and good searchlight work kept them from doing any widespread damage. East

Gladstone Dock was badly hit by a high-explosive and others damaged North-West Hornby Shed, railway trucks at No. 3 Alexandra Dock and Naval Stores, and North-West Gladstone Dock. More high-explosives fell in the Walton district, and there was damage to house property around Breeze Hill. One of the most poignant memories of that night is of a frail old lady who, as daylight came, was discovered by passers-by sitting in an armchair on the pavement outside her shattered home. "I am guarding the furniture until my husband returns with a cart to remove it," she told them. When a row of houses was wrecked the sole survivor was a baby. The infant was found, covered with soot, in front of a fireplace on the ground-floor. An overturned armchair had protected it from the falling debris. The child's parents lay dead at the other end of the room.

There were three more smallish raids on Liverpool in 1941 - on June 25th, July 24th and November 1st. The damage was slight, and in all three raids only two people were injured.

On Saturday, January 10th, 1942, the last bombs - a stick of four high-explosives - fell on Liverpool. They demolished five houses in Upper Stanhope Street and damaged many others in the vicinity. That was the last sting of the Luftwaffe and it brought death to fifteen people. Ten were killed outright, and five more were trapped and lost their lives beneath fallen masonry. Rescue work went on unremittingly over the weekend and a number of persons were brought out alive. Plucky work was done by members of the N.F.S. and two army sergeants. One of those who happened to be on the scene at the time of the incident was Auxiliary Fireman J.E. Jones, who had already been awarded the B.E.M. for his work during the May Blitz. With the assistance of the two sergeants and Auxiliary Fireman Harry Condie, he succeeded in rescuing several of the trapped people, including a 70-year-old woman whose foot had been caught in a blown-out-fire-grate. That was the night, too, when the newly-formed Home Guard A.A. batteries on Merseyside got the chance they had been eagerly awaiting to go into action, and they made history as the first Home Guard A.A. batteries in the country to fire at Nazi raiders. They were never called upon again for, so far as Merseyside was concerned, that January night of 1942 marked the end of a holocaust.

And holocaust is surely the only word which adequately describes all that Merseyside had endured: 509 alerts; 68 raids; 119 land-mines; 2,315 high-explosive, 50 oil, and innumerable incendiary bombs dropped on Liverpool alone. Out of a total of 282,000 Merseyside homes, 184,300 damaged and 10,840 destroyed.

Liverpool could pause now and look back upon the dark days of its most bitter ordeal. It could see how determination had triumphed over difficulty. It could even find time to laugh, for there were moments of humour to remember, too. That moment on the morning of Sunday, May 4th, 1941, for example, when, after the shattering raid of the Saturday night, a Regional Commissioner's Conference was called in order to decide how best to meet the emergency. The Regional Commissioner, Sir Harry Haig, together with naval, military and air-force chiefs and the heads of all Liverpool's various civil defence services were gathered in a large room in the Municipal Annexe, when suddenly the door opened and a little man bearing a short ladder on his shoulder walked unconcernedly, beneath the amazed stares of all the assembled brass, across to the clock. without as much as a single glance at the gaping company, he produced a key from his trousers pocket and proceeded calmly to wind the clock. The city lay in smoking ruins all about, but that little man had been winding that clock at 11 a.m. every Sunday morning for years and years and he did not see why he should fail in his duty now. Time waits for no man. Life has to go on. And maybe as he walked quietly out of the conference chamber, his job done, those who remained behind found new heart as a result of the object lesson in carrying on under difficulties which had just been provided by that uninvited guest.

At a minute to midnight on August 9th, 1942, two years to the day since the Great Merseyside Blitz began with those six bombs screaming earthwards at Prenton, the now unfamiliar alert sounded. For the 500th time there were raiders over Merseyside. Flares were dropped over several Liverpool districts, including Norris Green, but there were no bombs. And at nineteen minutes past one in the early hours of the morning of August 10th, 1942, the 'All Clear' rang out over the cold wide estuary for the last time. No more the crouching in bomb-strafed shelters, ears straining to catch the quiverings of the wing-beats of death. No more the hopeless guessing games - guns or bombs? Theirs or ours?

In the early hours of September 15th, 1942, a minor echo of the days of the great raids was sounded when a barrage-balloon broke loose from its moorings and exploded, damaging houses in Kirkdale. A rest centre was opened for the 70 people rendered homeless until billets could be found for them.

But it *was* only an echo and, no longer under bombardment, Liverpool licked its wounds and soon the vital cargoes were being handled again with the old efficiency. Throughout the war Liverpool dealt with 75 million tons of cargo, including 73,000 aircraft and 19 million tons of food-stuffs, and 4,700,000 troops passed through the port. A North African landing force sailed from the Mersey. Many of the cumbrous segments of Mulberry Harbour were despatched from here to the beaches of Normandy. And Pluto, the famous fuel-pipe which stretched underwater to the battlefields of France, had its main terminal buoy in the river opposite Dingle. Merseyside was at last paying the Luftwaffe back.

But Liverpool's active participation in civil defence had not ceased with the last bomb. Flying bombs and rockets on the South led to wholesale evacuations in which Liverool played a part as host. Rest centres were opened for the reception of evacuees off trains pending their allocation to billets, and by October 1942, 350 such refugees had been accommodated here.

Presently the triumphant Allied armies were sweeping half across the world in pursuit of the hard-pressed forces of the Third Reich - Africa, Italy, the continent of Europe - and Hitler had neither the time nor the resources to spare for Britain - the Great Merseyside Blitz was over.

It belongs now to history. If this has seemed only a record of death and disaster, then I have failed in my assignment. Of course death and disaster were very much a part of the story, but there is more - so much more - to it than that. There is courage and heroism - oasis of good in the desert of Hitler's evil. The inspired bravery of unpremeditated acts of grace by individual soldiers in that great civilian army of civil defence workers - the Fourth Service which had more than justified its proud place alongside the Army, the Navy and the Air-Force in the victory parades that were to come. The less spectacular, but every bit as real courage of the nameless thousands who trudged night after night to the shelters, and whose only complaint was that cigarettes were scarce.

And now many years have gone by since they did, in the wistful words of the war-time song, sound the last 'All Clear,' The lights have gone on again all over the world. Why then dwell on past horrors? Why - even though reverently - drag it all up again? New houses and beautiful buildings have arisen, Phoenix-like, from the flames. Nature has drawn a gentle green coverlet over the black scars of the blitzed sites, and the human memory has played its old - and perhaps merciful - trick of forgetting. But that is precisely the point. WE MUST NOT FORGET. We must never forget, for if man's material progress continues to outpace his spiritual development, such a thing could happen again. We pray that it will not, but we must be prepared - just in case. We must not let the curtains of complacency fall upon our minds, nor allow fear of recollecting past heartbreaks to blind us to the necessity of anticipating possible future sorrows *and doing something about it.* A trained, alert body of civil defence personnel should exist even in the piping days of peace, for in a topsy-turvy world it is a strangely contradictory fact that one of the best ways of ensuring peace is to prepare for war.